From Creation to Canaan

From Creation to Canaan

Biblical Hermeneutics for the Anthropocene

MICK POPE

PICKWICK *Publications* • Eugene, Oregon

FROM CREATION TO CANAAN
Biblical Hermeneutics for the Anthropocene

Copyright © 2024 Mick Pope. All rights reserved. Except for brief quotations in critical publications or reviews, no part of this book may be reproduced in any manner without prior written permission from the publisher. Write: Permissions, Wipf and Stock Publishers, 199 W. 8th Ave., Suite 3, Eugene, OR 97401.

Pickwick Publications
An Imprint of Wipf and Stock Publishers
199 W. 8th Ave., Suite 3
Eugene, OR 97401

www.wipfandstock.com

PAPERBACK ISBN: 978-1-6667-5145-1
HARDCOVER ISBN: 978-1-6667-5146-8
EBOOK ISBN: 978-1-6667-5147-5

Cataloguing-in-Publication data:

Names: Pope, Mick [author].

Title: From creation to Canaan : biblical hermeneutics for the anthropocene / Mick Pope.

Description: Eugene, OR: Pickwick Publications, 2024 | Includes bibliographical references and index.

Identifiers: ISBN 978-1-6667-5145-1 (paperback) | ISBN 978-1-6667-5146-8 (hardcover) | ISBN 978-1-6667-5147-5 (ebook)

Subjects: LCSH: Human ecology—Biblical teaching. | Ecotheology. | Creation. | Bible.—Genesis, I.—Criticism, interpretations, etc. | Bible.—Leviticus, XVII–XXVU—Criticism, interpretation, etc. | Sabbath. | Eden. | Environmentalism—Religious aspects—Christianity.

Classification: BS660 P67 2024 (print) | BS660 (ebook)

Scripture quotations are from the Revised Standard Version of the Bible, copyright © 1946, 1952, and 1971 National Council of the Churches of Christ in the United States of America. Used by permission. All rights reserved worldwide.

Scripture quotations taken from the (NASB®) New American Standard Bible®, Copyright © 1960, 1971, 1977, 1995, 2020 by The Lockman Foundation. Used by permission. All rights reserved. www.lockman.org

Table of Contents

List of Illustrations vi

Preface vii

Acknowledgements ix

Introduction xi

1. The Anthropocene and Human Agency 1

2. Sabbath Keeping in H 24

3. The Holy Garden 56

4. The Ethical Anthropocene 85

Bibliography 97

Name Index 107

Subject Index 109

List of Illustrations

Figure 1. The generations of the *erets* leading to wild plants.

Figure 2. The generations of the *erets* leading to cultivated plants.

Figure 3. The generations of the *erets* leading to various living beings.

Preface

I GUESS I COULD say I am a degree collector. The book you are now holding is the result of nearly three and a half years of part time study towards a MPhil in Hebrew Bible. I'm not much of a Hebrew scholar, but here it is. At the time of publication, I am working on a PhD in systematic theology, picking up on themes developed here. This is on the back several degrees in science, including a PhD in meteorology. So why am I doing this? Not for bragging rights, although the pain and effort alone are worth talking about!

I have spent many years speaking and writing at a popular level about the present environmental crisis. Try being a meteorologist with some theology behind you, churches are soon queuing up to ask you what you think about climate change. Well, I *wish* they were queuing, but there have been enough opportunities with churches, aid and advocacy groups, and theological colleges, that I have not given up on the hope that what I am doing is useful to the church, and that the church is still willing to be useful to the world.

You would have to be in severe denial to not see that the future of our planet is dire, or else perhaps lacking compassion for the millions who are already suffering. Or perhaps plain lucky that you have not been inconvenienced as the impacts of climate change unfold. Now more than ever, we need to be, as the church, those in the front line, loving our neighbors as ourselves. These are our neighbors in space, and no longer "out there" but sometimes right next door. I have taught meteorology to Pacific Islanders who can document their islands disappearing beneath the waves. I have gone to church with young people who have escaped extreme wildfires by coming home on the deck of a Navy vessel. But there are also our neighbors in time. After I am gone, what kind of world will my adult son establish his career, and possibly raise his own family in?

As you will see from the pages that follow, I believe that God has tasked us with caring for this world. This means not passively sitting back and waiting for history to end. In the beginning was a good creation, and even though God will bring it all to fruition, ours is the task of being involved. We can unleash or prevent chaos. It is perhaps a radical idea to some, but at least one part of the Hebrew tradition understands caring for the land to be an expression of holiness. It took me over three years of hard work to piece this idea together. I hope reading this book doesn't take you as long and makes that journey easier. More than that, I hope that the reward of digging deeper into a little corner of Scripture and doing the hard thinking as I have tried to do, changes the way you look at and treat the world around you. The alternative is chaos.

Acknowledgments

IN THE SPIRIT OF reconciliation, I acknowledge the Traditional Custodians of country throughout Australia and their connections to land, sea, and community. In particular, I acknowledge the Wurundjeri people of the Kulin nation here in Naarm/Melbourne where this manuscript was prepared. I pay my respect to their Elders past and present and extend that respect to all Aboriginal and Torres Strait Islander peoples today.

I also acknowledge the support of my supervisors, Prof. Mark Brett, and Rev. Assoc. Prof. Jason Goroncy. Without their help and guidance, this manuscript would not have been possible.

Introduction

THE ANTHROPOCENE IS AT once one of the most important and controversial concepts of the twenty-first century. This concept suggests that humanity has become a geological force affecting all aspects of the Earth system. While it is a useful tool for thinking about human impacts, it is not without its critics.[1] It obscures specific ideological, political, and economic factors. Notwithstanding these problems, I propose it remains valuable for considering both the existential threat to humanity that the current environmental crisis poses, and the challenges to basic assumptions of modern thought, including theological ones.

The Anthropocene challenges the culture/nature dualism, including the idea that human agency is unique, and that individual human action is disconnected from wider consequences.[2] It also represents a confrontation of two dramatically dissimilar timeframes: human history grounded in "processual change of modern (Western) historical sensibility," and geological history which presents us with unprecedented changes which challenges the "ontic certainty" of the world.[3] Clive Hamilton believes these unprecedented changes mean that no previous cultural learning can prepare us to deal with them.[4] However, Schmidt, Brown, and Orr warn that rejecting traditional ethics for scientific reasons risks a

1. See, for example, Moore, *Anthropocene or Capitalocene?*
2. Schmidt et al., "Ethics in the Anthropocene," 188–200.
3. Bińczyk, "Most Unique Discussion," 4; Simon, "Why the Anthropocene Has No History," 242; Chakrabarty, "Anthropocene Time," 31.
4. Hamilton et al., *Anthropocene and the Global Environmental Crisis*, 5.

INTRODUCTION

recapitulation of the colonial privileging of western perspectives.[5] They see a role for a more benign form of anthropocentrism in the exercise of this power, which the Abrahamic faiths may inform.[6]

Their line of argument prompts me to return to the Primeval History (Gen 1–11, especially the creation narratives) and to the Holiness Code (Lev 17–26), and to inquire what these texts might teach about human responsibility for creation, humanity's relationship to and with creation, and about notions of mastery and control. Essentially, two questions are addressed. First, what was Israel's responsibility for the land in these texts, and how was this linked to their understanding of divine sovereignty and to the nature of the land itself? Secondly, how might an understanding of this responsibility impact on religious communities who continue to acknowledge this text as Scripture?

The first of these questions is addressed by engaging in exegesis of the Hebrew text. In dialogue with recent research, I will argue that Genesis 1:1—2:3 is the work of the Holiness school (H), reworking an earlier Priestly (P) account.[7] Three themes of importance for the present work are then subsequently brought together by H in Leviticus 17–26.

The first theme is that of the creation of sacred space. Genesis 1:1—2:3 describes the creation of a protological temple. With P's Flood narrative, it forms a *chaoskampf* or struggle against chaos. In ancient Near Eastern myth, such a struggle if followed by the enthronement of a deity in a temple. While in P this comes with the completion of the Tabernacle (Exod 40), the non-P Garden story links Eden with the Jerusalem temple, and Earth care with sacral kingship. In Leviticus, one might say, H Edenizes all of Canaan. In chapter 4, I argue for the possibility of Edenizing the whole earth.

The second theme is that of the Sabbath and the creation of sacred time. Genesis 1:1—2:3 is an etiological account of the Sabbath. The subduing of chaos in the *chaoskampf* is celebrated by declaring sacred time in setting apart the seventh day as holy. In

---

5. Schmidt et al., "Ethics in the Anthropocene," 191.
6. Schmidt et al., "Ethics in the Anthropocene," 194.
7. The composition of Gen 2:4 will be given special attention in chapter 3.

INTRODUCTION

Leviticus, the Sabbath underpins the Israelite agrarian economy. The themes of Sabbath and sanctuary from Genesis 1–3 are brought together by H as central aspects of lay Israelite holiness, including their responsibility to give Sabbath rest to the land. Grounding Sabbath in the creation narrative allows the possibility of Sabbath to be associated with a universal Earth-care ethic, at least for those who receive such texts as, in some sense at least, authoritative.

Finally, there is the theme of the Earth/land of Israel, both referred to by the Hebrew *erets*. In Genesis 1:1—2:3, the Earth has agency to take an active part in its own unfolding. All of creation appears to share in the rest of the seventh day. Leviticus further develops this theology of the agency of the *erets*. Just as the Earth as *erets* is fashioned by God as a temple to dwell in, so *Yhwh* has a relationship with the land as *erets* that predates that of Israel. The land is to enjoy and to keep its own Sabbath, just as Genesis suggests. Likewise, just as P's Flood represents chaos released on all flesh due violence on the Earth, the land can unleash chaos on the people for covenant violation, vomiting them out.

When it comes to the relevance of this exegetical discussion for communities of faith, the land's role in divine judgement is consonant with Michael Northcott's understanding of the character of divine justice being written into the Earth, as we shall see especially in chapter 4, after a detailed discussion of both creation narratives in Genesis. The recognition of non-human agency allows possible linkages with Earth jurisprudence and postcolonial readings of Scripture. The first chapter introduces the concept of the Anthropocene as developed in the natural sciences, together with some of the criticisms raised in the environmental humanities. It identifies some of the challenges the concept creates for modern thought, including a theological marriage between forms of millennialism and western capitalism. We return to these larger questions about the Anthropocene in chapter 4, reflecting on the significance of the exegetical work on Holiness theology in Genesis and Leviticus.

I

The Anthropocene and Human Agency

The Anthropocene

Defining the Anthropocene

THE TERM ANTHROPOCENE ENTERED modern parlance via the work of atmospheric chemist Paul Crutzen, although it has a longer historical pedigree.[1] While Crutzen identifies the beginning of the Anthropocene with the start of the Industrial Revolution, the generally accepted definition of the Anthropocene aligns with a period known as the "Great Acceleration," beginning around 1950. Viewed as a new geological era, the Anthropocene represents a departure from the Holocene. Beginning about 11,700 years ago, the Holocene was an interglacial period with a warm and relatively stable climate, compared to the cold and highly variable conditions of the preceding Pleistocene.[2] This climate stability provided the conditions for the rise of civilization, with city states, agriculture, written languages, stratified cultures, and the axial religions.

---

1. Crutzen, "Geology of Mankind," 23. For a discussion of older uses of the term, see Bonneuil and Fressoz, *Shock of the Anthropocene*.

2. Wallace and Hobbs, *Atmospheric Science*, 55.

The geological signature of the Anthropocene is a spike in radioactive Carbon-14, associated with nuclear weapons testing.[3] Will Steffen and co-authors observe a relatively slow increase in socio-economic trends from 1750 up until this time. A rapid acceleration then occurs in global population, urbanization, gross domestic product, primary energy use, fertilizer use, fresh water use, and dam building. Organisation for Economic Co-operation and Development (OECD) countries dominate all these statistics, apart from human population.[4] Concomitant with these trends have been changes in various aspects of the Earth system. These changes are measured against nine planetary boundaries, which represent the Holocene conditions under which human society evolved and has flourished. Steffen and co-authors refer to this as our "safe operating space."[5] Each of these boundaries are discussed briefly below.

Measuring the Anthropocene

Climate change is the best known and understood of the planetary boundaries. Natural climate variability occurs due to internal changes in the atmosphere and oceans and is driven by changes in the distribution of solar heating.[6] Anthropogenic climate change is caused by the burning of fossil fuels and changes in land use. The overuse of fertilizers and production of cement also contribute.

---

3. The Anthropocene is not recognized by the International Commission on Stratigraphy. For the latest version of the International Chronostratigraphic chart that indicates the accepted geological periods, see International Union of Geological Scientists, "International Chronostratigraphic Chart."

4. Steffen et al., "Trajectory of the Anthropocene," 1–18.

5. Steffen et al., "Planetary Boundaries."

6. An example of an atmosphere-ocean interaction that drives climate variability is the Atlantic Meridional Overturning Circulation, which produces glaciation events over the Northern Hemisphere. For a recent discussion, see Muschitiello et al., "Deep-Water Circulation." The distribution of solar radiation over Earth's surface are driven by changes in Earth's orbit, known as Milankovich cycles. For a general summary, see Maslin, "Forty Years of Linking Orbits to Ice Ages," 208–9.

The resultant warming of the atmosphere and oceans modifies weather patterns, increases the height of the oceans, and melts ice caps. The measure for this boundary is the concentration of atmospheric carbon dioxide, a major greenhouse gas. Atmospheric concentrations have increased from a pre-industrial 280 part per million (ppm), to over 420 ppm in January 2024[7] A suggested safe threshold is 350 ppm.[8]

Carbon dioxide not only raises the global temperature, but when mixed with ocean water also raises its acidity. A 2012 study found a thirty-fold increase in the natural variation in ocean acidity in the Pacific and Caribbean oceans since the beginning of the Industrial Revolution. This increase was associated with a decline in coral growth rates of 15 percent over pre-industrial levels, threatening tourism revenues and food security, among other things.[9]

The iconic dodo (*Raphus cucullatus*) reminds us that humans can cause animal species to disappear over a relatively short period of time.[10] Current extinction rates are unprecedented, although using extinction as a "planetary boundary" is problematic, and not without its critics.[11] Estimates of extinction rates can vary wildly, but the best estimates are at least 100 times the long term background extinction rate.[12] This has led some to dub the present ecological crisis the sixth mass extinction event.[13] Steffen and

---

7. For current levels, see NOAA Global Monitoring Laboratory, "Trends in Atmospheric Carbon Dioxide."

8. Hansen et al., "Target Atmospheric CO_2," 217–31.

9. Friedrich et al., "Detecting Regional Anthropogenic Trends," 167–71.

10. See, for example, Fuller, *Dodo*.

11. Montoya et al., "Planetary Boundary," 234.

12. The background extinction rate represents the rate of extinction that typifies geological history, in contrast to both natural mass extinctions, and those due to human activity. For a recent estimate, see De Vos et al., "Estimating the Normal Background Rate," 152–62.

13. Compared to the previous five mass extinction events, including the death of the dinosaurs due to a large meteorite impact and the so-called "Great dying" caused by prolonged volcanic activity. See Kolbert, *Sixth Extinction*.

co-authors define the extinction boundary in terms of reduced genetic variability and impoverished ecosystems.[14]

Both animal and human wellbeing are threatened by artificial chemicals. Rachel Carson made the pesticide DDT infamous with her book *Silent Spring*, where it was implicated in the death of North American birds.[15] Its use was banned in Australia in 1987, and after twenty years a dramatic increase in the reproductive success of peregrine falcons has been observed.[16] It is estimated that there are some one hundred thousand novel entities in global commerce today, substances that have "the potential for unwanted geophysical and/or biological effects."[17] Plastics are slow to decay, and large pieces kill thousands of sea birds every year.[18] Small particles, known as microplastics, can pollute soil, kill earthworms, and contaminate drinking water.[19]

Industrial fertilizers, yet another family of artificial chemicals used extensively, are disrupting the Earth system. Damage has been done to waterways due to the over-application of nitrogen and phosphorus-based fertilizers. For example, overuse in China increased soil nitrogen by 60 percent between 1980 and 2010.[20] Nitrogen can fertilise algal growth, producing toxic blooms. When the algae die, their decay consumes oxygen, producing anoxic or dead zones.[21]

The availability of potable water is declining due to changes in rainfall patterns, pollution, and overuse. In south-eastern Australia, wintertime rainfall has been in decline for several decades. Both ozone loss and warming polar temperatures have produced a

---

14. Steffen et al., *Planetary Boundaries*, 5.
15. Carson, *Silent Spring*.
16. See Jess, "DDT Environmental Effects."
17. Steffen et al., *Planetary Boundaries*, 7.
18. Savoca et al., "Marine Plastic Debris."
19. Boots et al., "Effects of Microplastics in Soil Ecosystems," 1149–506; Oßmann, "Microplastics in Drinking Water?," 44–51.
20. Liu et al., "Enhanced Nitrogen Deposition over China," 459–62.
21. Hughes et al., "Climate Mediates Hypoxic Stress," 8025–30.

southward shift in the track of frontal systems.[22] Extraction of gas by the fracking process has been implicated in the contamination of drinking water in the USA.[23] Many parts of the world face possible depleted underground aquifers by mid-century due to over extraction for agriculture.[24] Rivers can also become depleted. The Murray Darling Basin in eastern Australia is an example of such overuse and mismanagement.[25]

Land system changes, typically associated with large-scale agriculture, modify several planetary boundaries. Loss of tropical rainforest reduces local precipitation by reducing evapotranspiration from vegetation. These changes can further affect global weather patterns. Grasslands and agricultural land also store less carbon than do forested areas, contributing to climate change, while habitat loss contributes to species extinction.[26]

Atmospheric aerosols reduce air quality, and result in approximately 7.2 million deaths per year. The sources of these includes industry, combustion engines, wildfires, and solid fuel burning for cooking.[27] India has fourteen of the world's most polluted cities. About half of Delhi's 4.4 million schoolchildren have stunted lung development.[28] Climate change is increasing the frequency of wildfires, with its associated impacts on air quality. In Sydney, during Australia's December 2019 bushfires, the air quality index was three times worse than any time in the preceding five-year period.[29]

---

22. Hendon et al., "Seasonal Variations," 3446–60.

23. Jackson et al., "Depths of Hydraulic Fracturing," 8969–76.

24. Aquifers are underground layers of water-bearing permeable rock that can be accessed using wells. Rad et al., "Downside Risk of Aquifer Depletion," 577–91.

25. Davies, "Murray-Darling Basin Plan"; Slezak and Davies, "Murray-Darling Water Theft Allegations."

26. Steffen et al., *Planetary Boundaries*, 7.

27. Steffen et al., *Planetary Boundaries*, 7.

28. Siddique et al., "Air Pollution," 89–100.

29. Judd and Taylor, "Smoke and Bushfires."

The last planetary boundary provides some climate and environmental activists with encouragement, as it demonstrates the potential success of global cooperation. Over 35 years ago, the Montreal Protocol (1987) resulted in the phasing out of industrial gases such as chlorofluorocarbons (CFCs), which contributed to the so-called "hole" in the ozone layer. These chemicals react with ozone in the very cold clouds that occur over the earth's poles during winter. The region of lower ozone concentration produced as a result has a hole-like appearance on satellite imagery. With the onset of spring, this ozone-poor air is circulated away from the poles. Since the signing of the Protocol, concentrations have been recovering.[30]

The Rapidly Changing Anthropocene

While the Anthropocene can be measured with reference to planetary boundaries, it is not only the passing of such boundaries that is significant, but also the rate at which this occurs. One way of conceptualizing the rapidity of such changes is Gaffney and Steffen's "Anthropocene equation."[31] This equation represents a simple heuristic for understanding changes as a function of astrophysical, geophysical, internal, and anthropogenic processes. Astrophysical factors here include the long-term brightening of the sun, shorter term solar variability (such as sunspot cycles), meteorite impacts, and changes to the Earth's orbit. Geophysical factors include volcanic eruptions, and the movement and growth of continents. Unforced internal variability in atmospheric motions and ocean currents is also observed.

Gaffney and Steffen show that rates of change due to human influence are larger than natural processes observed over long timescales. For example, the rate of increase of atmospheric carbon dioxide concentrations from 1970 to 2015 is about 550 times larger

---

30. Solomon et al., "Emergence of Healing," 269–74. For recent observations of ozone concentrations, see NASA Goddard Space Flight Centre, "NASA Ozone Watch."

31. Gaffney and Steffen, "Anthropocene Equation," 53–61.

than the Holocene base rate, and 100 times that observed during the last glacial termination.[32] Global temperature rises during the period 1970 to 2015 were 170 times faster than the Holocene base rate. Natural processes have kept the Earth system oscillating between glacial and interglacial periods. However, human influences are pushing the Earth towards "Hothouse earth."[33] At a threshold of about 2°C above pre-industrial levels, internal feedback mechanisms will begin to cause irreversible changes known as tipping points. Such changes include the loss of the Greenland Icesheet and the collapse of the Amazon rainforest.[34]

Historical Stages of the Anthropocene

While most discussions of the scientific research on the Anthropocene centers on the Great Acceleration, this event did not appear *ex nihilo*. The Great Acceleration provides a datable geological marker to potentially satisfy the requirements of defining a new geological era. However, unlike preceding geological eras, the Anthropocene is the result of human action, not non-human biological or geological processes. Even if the Great Acceleration is a sufficient geological definition of the Anthropocene, other historical transitions may better inform our understanding of the ideological origins. In particular, the dating the origins of the Anthropocene raises theological questions around human agency. Was the beginning of the Anthropocene unintentional and hence unavoidable, the result of deliberate choices driven by particular ideologies, or a more complex combination of these two extremes? Is human agency sufficient to navigate our collective way through the present existential crisis?

---

32. A glacial termination as the phrase suggests, occurs when glaciers melt due to rising global temperatures.

33. Steffen et al., "Trajectories of the Earth System," 8252–59.

34. For a recent discussion of the risk of the Amazon rainforest transitioning to savannah, see Staal et al., "Hysteresis of Tropical Forests," 1–8.

Simon Lewis and Mark Maslin have tracked the origins of the modern Anthropocene through four proceeding stages.[35] The first stage is the Pleistocene extinctions of large-bodied mammals (or megafauna), concomitant with human migration out of Africa between about fifty thousand to ten thousand years ago. These extinctions are typically ascribed to the so-called "overkill hypothesis."[36] In this hypothesis, human cognitive ability, demonstrated in our ability to make tools, cooperate in groups, and form a theory of mind for prey animals, led to overhunting.[37] It is likely that human beings would not have become a geological force in the modern period without these cognitive abilities, and these extinction events are a marker of this. However, as a formal definition of Anthropocene onset, the megafaunal extinctions are problematic. As Lewis and Maslin note, the timing of these extinctions is asynchronous, tracking human migration patterns.[38] The overkill hypothesis is also not universally applicable. Recent archaeological discoveries in Australia place the arrival of humans before the local extinction of megafauna. Long cohabitation times makes a primary anthropogenic cause of megafaunal extinctions in Australia less likely.[39] An implication might be that the Anthropocene is not a necessary part of the human condition. Our cognitive abilities are a necessary but not sufficient condition for the Anthropocene.

The second historical stage is the origin and intensification of farming, with its associated land clearing and resulting greenhouse gas emissions. Lewis and Maslin describe farming as the first energy revolution. The energy demands for a subsistence farming life were greater than that of a hunter-gather lifestyle by more than a factor of six. At the same time, energy extraction from

---

35. Lewis and Maslin, "Defining the Anthropocene," 171–80; Lewis and Maslin, *Human Planet*.
36. See, for example, Nagaoka et al., "Overkill Model," 9683–96.
37. Lewis and Maslin, *Human Planet*, 97–100.
38. Lewis and Maslin, *Human Planet*, 101–7.
39. Westaway et al., "At Least 17,000 Years of Coexistence," 206–11.

the biosphere increased from less than 0.01 percent to about 3 percent.[40] The present scale of agriculture is such that domesticated animals represent about 60 percent of the Earth's total biomass, compared to 36 percent for humans and 4 percent for wild animals.[41]

Modern humans appeared about two hundred thousand years ago, but agriculture only began with the onset of the Holocene. Pleistocene conditions were colder and drier than those of the Holocene. Lower CO_2 levels resulted in lower potential crop yields. While changes in the Earth's orbit produced a warmer, wetter climate, with increased CO_2 levels, Bill Ruddiman argues that agriculture has helped maintain these conditions.[42] Land clearing for agriculture resulted in rising CO_2 levels from about seven thousand years ago. The adoption of wet rice agriculture some five thousand years ago has likewise increased methane levels. The net effect has kept the atmosphere above the 240 ppm CO_2 threshold for the return to ice age conditions.[43] Agriculture is a contributor to the modern Anthropocene, together with forestry and other land uses, producing 13 percent of CO_2 emission, 44 percent of methane emissions, and 81 percent of nitrous oxide emissions.[44] However, these emissions have been driven both by population growth and changes in per capita consumption of food.[45] Neither of these is inevitable, but are driven by other underlying factors.

The third stage of the evolution of the Anthropocene is the European invasion of the Americas, beginning in 1492.[46] The Columbian Exchange involved the movement of human foodstuffs between the "Old" and "New" worlds. This included plants and livestock, as well as accidental transfers of pest species such as

---

40. Lewis and Maslin, *Human Planet*, 115–16.

41. Lewis and Maslin, *Human Planet*, 129. Bar-On et al., "Biomass Distribution on Earth," 6506–11.

42. Ruddiman, *Plows, Plagues, and Petroleum*.

43. Lewis and Maslin, *Human Planet*, 144.

44. IPCC, "Summary for Policymakers," 11.

45. IPCC, "Summary for Policymakers," 7.

46. Lewis and Maslin, *Human Planet*, chapter 5.

rats and earthworms. Apart from modifying human diets and disturbing ecosystem compositions, Europeans introduced diseases that the Indigenous peoples had no immunity to.[47] Together with war, slavery, and famine, the Indigenous population collapsed. Pre-contact estimates range from fifty-four to sixty-one million people, with a reduction to about six million by 1650. Over fifty million hectares of farmland reverted to natural vegetation, producing a dip of 7–10 ppm in CO_2 by 1610, known as the Orbis spike. Orbis comes from the Latin for world, carrying both the meaning of the unification of hemispheres and the beginning of a new world system. The Columbian Exchange may be considered as one phase of the overall tendency for humans to transfer species consciously or otherwise. This transfer has effectively created a supercontinent, referred to as New Pangea, where species may freely migrate.[48] As will be made clearer below, this period marks the ideological beginnings of the modern Anthropocene.

The last stage preceding the Great Acceleration was the beginning of the Industrial Revolution, which began around 1760.[49] The onset of this period was accompanied by an increase in coal burning. The resultant emissions of the greenhouse gas carbon dioxide are captured in polar ice cores. Crutzen suggests that the beginning of the Industrial Revolution marked the start of the Anthropocene when he introduced the term.[50] However, there is no clearly defined spike in carbon dioxide emissions that could be taken as a geological marker as Lewis and Maslin observe. Little impact on emissions is observed until the nineteenth century, and then a slow and steady increase is observed until the Great Acceleration. Therefore, while not a satisfactory definition of the Anthropocene, the Industrial Revolution is clearly a necessary step towards its development in the Great Acceleration, which is reliant upon cheap energy from fossil fuels.

---

47. Lindenau et al., "Distribution Patterns of Variability," 177–85.
48. Lewis and Maslin, *Human Planet*, 164–68.
49. Lewis and Maslin, "Defining the Anthropocene," 175.
50. Crutzen, "Geology of Mankind," 23.

Was the Anthropocene Inevitable?

Each stage outlined above was a necessary pre-cursor for the onset of the Anthropocene in the Great Acceleration. However, this begs the question of whether each of those historical stages were sufficient conditions for the emergence of the Anthropocene. Was the Great Acceleration inevitable? Do large-brained primates necessarily have to evolve into environmentally destructive creatures? Do the cognitive abilities of language, sociality, organization, and tool making, lead inevitably to the self-destruction of the species that possesses them?

Astrophysicist Adam Frank argues that the Anthropocene is merely a stage of the development of civilization that the human creature must pass through, as we learn to harvest the energy of the entire planet.[51] The lesson we are to learn is that our civilization has ignored potential feedbacks from the Earth system as we harvest this energy. He argues that our connectivity to the biosphere is the fact that "every civilization must be seen as a new form of biospheric activity arising from a planet's history of transformation and evolutionary innovation."[52] In other words, the Anthropocene is simply another period of geohistory, arising from the emergence of human civilization via evolution.

Frank takes an optimistic approach to the Anthropocene by positing the likelihood of multiple civilizations in an astrophysical context. Even making the most pessimistic assumptions about the origins of life elsewhere in the galaxy, and its evolution to intelligence, it is still likely that other civilizations exist. Each of these civilizations living on exoplanets (planets outside our solar system) will inevitably face their own version of the Anthropocene. Frank then bases his optimism on assuming that statistically, at least one species should be able to survive the Anthropocene, and that this may include our own species.[53]

---

51. Frank, *Light of the Stars*.
52. Frank, *Light of the Stars*, 213.
53. Frank, *Light of the Stars*, 219.

Not all scholars share such speculative optimism. Philosopher Nick Bostrom, for example, considers the development of civilizations as consisting of "one or more *highly improbable* evolutionary transitions," which includes the tendency for self-destruction.[54] Evidence of the potential for self-destruction in one species, *Homo Sapiens*, is apparent in the Anthropocene. Bostrom's argument is the reverse of that of Frank. If it is statistically unlikely that civilizations will survive their own Anthropocene, this makes our own survival also less likely. Both Frank and Bostrom assume that the Anthropocene is either a necessary stage of evolution, or in some sense unavoidable. Such claims should provoke us to reflect more deeply on the implications of human mastery over nature, whether as the cause of, or the road through, the Anthropocene.

The Problem of Human Agency

Anthropocene, Capitalocene, and Human Agency

The arrival of the Anthropocene demonstrates that the Baconian narrative of "mastery over nature," is largely illusory, because while humanity has been able to manipulate nature for its own ends, the results of this manipulation have exceeded our control.[55] The flourishing of human civilization, and the concomitant development of technology, has in turn undermined the very basis on which it is built. Establishing responsibility for the impacts on the Earth system during the Anthropocene is problematic. It is the result of many small choices taken by individuals, communities, governments, corporations, and others, which cumulatively have a large—and possibly irreversible—impact.[56]

The distributed nature of human choice does not remove the problem of individual responsibility, however. Rather it makes it more difficult to ascribe blame in many cases. However, this does not imply that all human actions have been undertaken in

---

54. Bostrom, "Where Are They?," 72–77.
55. See Schmidt et al., "Ethics in the Anthropocene," 190.
56. Schmidt et al., "Ethics in the Anthropocene," 192.

ignorance of their larger consequences, or that there are not particular individuals or collectives that do not bear a disproportionate share of blame. This hinges on two simple facts: First, scientists have been warning human society about the perils of climate change for over a century. In 1908, Svante Arrhenius, a Swedish chemist who was awarded a Nobel Prize in 1903, warned that a doubling of CO_2 concentrations will lead to 4°C of warming.[57] He anticipated an increase in the acidity of the oceans over the course of a few centuries, given the rates of fossil fuel burning in his day.[58] And over fifty years ago, United States president Lyndon Johnson was warned by scientists of risks of increasing emissions.[59]

Secondly, these warnings have been consistently downplayed or ignored by many powerful special interest groups and politicians. Scientists at oil and gas multinational Exxon, for example, apparently knew about climate change forty years ago. However, Exxon has been implicated in funding think tanks such as the American Enterprise Institute, which actively obscures the science.[60] Naomi Oreskes and Erik Conway have documented the broader misinformation campaign in the United States, while Clive Hamilton has argued that Australian energy policy has been shaped by fossil fuel interests.[61] The engine of capitalism is fossil fuels, and hence the logic of capitalism dictates that fossil fuel use must continue, regardless of the impacts.[62]

---

57. Ahhrenius, *Worlds in the Making*, 53.

58. Ahhrenius, *Worlds in the Making*, 54.

59. The Environmental Pollution Panel, *Restoring the Quality of Our Environment*.

60. See Hall, "Exxon Knew about Climate Change." On denial, see Sachs, "How the AEI Distorts the Climate Debate." On funding of AEI by big oil see, Sample, "Scientists Offered Cash to Dispute Climate Study."

61. Oreskes and Conway, *Merchants of Doubt*; Hamilton, *Scorcher*.

62. The major contributors to the Anthropocene are the wealthy OECD countries. See Steffen et al., "Trajectory of the Anthropocene," 3. On the need for cheap energy to drive capitalism and the resultant environmental impacts, see Moore, "Rise of Cheap Nature," 78–115. On capitalism and climate change, see Gleeson-White, *Six Capitals*.

While then human agency may be exercised unconsciously or consciously of the impacts on the Earth, Dipesh Chakrabarty argues that the Anthropocene reminds us that our agency is not unique. Agency in the Earth system, he observes, is distributed in "Earth processes, technology, humans and other species." Unlike humans, non-human agency is not exercised consciously. Chakrabarty describes geological history as "a narrative of many dispersed and networked actors, none acting with the sense of internal autonomy with which humanist historians suffuse the word 'agency.'"[63] The geological processes that produced the prolonged volcanic activity which led to the end-Permian extinction some 252 million years ago was in no sense conscious of wiping out over 96 percent of life. Most humans are unlikely to be aware of being implicated in the sixth mass extinction.[64] However, because, as a species, human beings are agents capable of making conscious decisions with moral implications, we can assign moral responsibility to many individuals, and the political and economic systems of which we are a part.

The term Capitalocene identifies the logic of the Anthropocene in capitalism.[65] While the Anthropocene identifies humanity as a collective actor, the Capitalocene identifies industrialised nations as the specific cause of the changes to the Earth system we observe, as well as the origin of the underlying ideology.[66] Jason Moore observes that prior to 1450, ecological transformations took hundreds, if not thousands of years. After 1450, these transformations were measured in decades. The age of Capital (1450–1750) was defined by new technology, cheap nature, and cheap labor. The number of slaves disembarking each decade in the Americas, to grow sugar, increased 1065 percent between 1560

---

63. Chakrabarty, "Anthropocene Time," 25.

64. Kolbert, *Sixth Extinction*.

65. On defining the Capitalocene, see Moore, "Rise of Cheap Nature," 78–115; Chwałczyk, "Around the Anthropocene in Eighty Names," 4458. On the link between settler colonialism and the Anthropocene, see Davis and Todd, "On the Importance of a Date," 761–80.

66. Moore, "Rise of Cheap Nature," 82.

and 1710.[67] With the conquering of more than four million square kilometers between 1535 and 1680, the appropriation of the "New World" was fundamental to capitalism.[68]

This appropriation took the form of settler colonialism, which is ecocidal, transforming the earth by extraction and accumulation via a process of dispossession. This transformation is the deliberate intention, rather than being simply a by-product, of modernity. The dispossession and severing of relationship between people and soil in the apocalyptic genocide in the Americas, for example, is a preview of life in the Anthropocene. Insofar as settler colonialism led to the transformation of landscapes and forced displacement in many parts of the world, contemporary climate change can be seen as a direct continuation of the logic of colonialism.[69]

This cheapening of both nature and the human other as cheap labor leads Justin McBrien to identify the Necrocene as the Capitalocene's shadowy double. The Necrocene relates human agency exercised in capitalism, capital accumulation and negative-value in the form of deforestation, greenhouse gas emissions, and extinctions.[70]

We are thoroughly connected to other actors, human and non-human, a fact that capitalism ignores, or at least reduces to extraction and production. Chakrabarty notes that all actors are "always in a relationship of synecdoche to the distributed agency of the Earth processes."[71] In the Capitalocene, these relationships may be represented by the negative-value that capital accumulation produces. Hence, Ewa Bińczyk defines human hyperagency as our ability as a species to change the climate, while still being "enmeshed in the process of planetary metabolism." This metabolism is turning against us, as the nurturing "mother Earth"

---

67. Moore, "Rise of Cheap Nature," 98–99.
68. Moore, "Rise of Cheap Nature," 102.
69. Davis and Todd, "On the Importance of a Date," 770–71. For a theological examination, see Jennings, *Christian Imagination*.
70. McBrien, "Accumulating Extinction," 116–18.
71. Chakrabarty, "Anthropocene Time," 28.

becomes the "uncontrollable Other."[72] Clive Hamilton believes the unprecedented changes in this metabolism mean that no previous cultural learning can prepare us to deal with them.[73] This includes all Holocene religions.[74] Before countering Hamilton's charge in subsequent chapters, it must be acknowledged that some forms of Christianity are certainly guilty of such shortcomings. In particular, one must acknowledge the shortcomings in American Evangelicalism and apocalypticism that have aligned with capitalism in reinforcing the problem of the Anthropocene/Capitalocene.

Evangelical Christianity

David Bebbington differentiates Evangelicalism from other Christian traditions by four categories of belief: biblicism, crucicentrisim, conversionism, and evangelism.[75] In the United States, Evangelicalism is associated with a lack of engagement with, or rejection of, climate change science. A 2015 study by the Pew Research Centre found that white Evangelicals were more likely to associated global warming with natural cycles than human activity, or reject the evidence of warming.[76] Wylie Carr and co-authors conducted interviews with pastors and laity in Dallas, Texas, to further explore the reasons for Evangelical climate scepticism.[77] Each of the interviewees brought up at least one of the five theological ideas: biblical inerrancy; God's sovereignty; human sinfulness; evangelism; eschatology.[78]

---

72. Bińczyk, "Most Unique Discussion of the 21st Century?," 7–8.

73. Hamilton et al., *Anthropocene and the Global Environmental Crisis*, 5.

74. Some attempts have been made to address hyperagency from a theological perspective. See, for example, Ward, "Wealthy Hyperagency in a Throwaway Culture," 77–90. Also Szaj, "Hermeneutics at the Time of the Anthropocene," 235–54; Kahane, "Mastery without Mystery," 355–68.

75. Bebbington, *Evangelicalism in Modern Britain*.

76. Funk and Alper, *Religion and Science*, 33.

77. Carr et al., "Faithful Skeptics," 276–99.

78. Carr et al., "Faithful Skeptics," 283.

Inerrancy is employed to deny the significance of climate change. The interviewee Julie claims that "The ice caps have already all melted and submerged the earth," and "God said, 'I'll never flood the earth again ....' So in that regard, I cannot believe in global warming as something that is going to affect the entire planet." Sea level rise contradicts her understanding of Gen 9:11–15. Other interviewees don't engage with climate change because it is not mentioned in the bible.[79] More broadly, literalistic interpretations of Genesis feed into the creation-evolution debate, and build a general distrust of science by some Evangelicals.[80] I will examine the Priestly Flood story in chapter 2 below.[81]

The idea of God's sovereignty acts as a barrier to climate action. One third of respondents to Carr and co-authors stated views along these lines: "I think that we've had warming and cooling, and we're going to do whatever God wants, and I don't think that human beings are going to make a big difference." Any attempt to deal with the problem is "man trying to play God."[82] Interviewees also express a "religiously grounded anthropocentrism." However, while God is fully in control, Evangelicals often express the view that God has entrusted humans with care of creation. The frequently used term is stewardship.[83] This framing presents an opportunity for engaging Evangelicals on environmental issues. Matthew Goldberg and co-authors found that protecting God's creation is a top reason for American Christians to reduce global warming, and that a stewardship framework produces "significant increases in pro-environmental and climate change beliefs."[84] I examine divine sovereignty and human responsibility in chapter 2.

Ideas of human sinfulness can reinforce concern about climate change. Ralph presents a typically literalistic reading of Genesis 2–3 to express why we have what he terms "global pollution."

---

79. Carr et al., "Faithful Skeptics," 286.
80. Carr et al., "Faithful Skeptics," 287.
81. See also Pope, "Sea Is Eating the Ground," 79–92.
82. Carr et al., "Faithful Skeptics," 288.
83. Carr et al., "Faithful Skeptics," 289.
84. Goldberg et al., "Social Identity Approach," 442–63.

He states that "Before Adam and Eve sinned in the Garden of Eden, Christ created creation in shalom, perfect peace and perfect harmony." Sin is then introduced, leading to the current climate crisis. The doctrine of sin can also provide a counterbalance to divine sovereignty implying that humans can't affect the global climate. Camden argues that while God is in control, humans also exercise freedom to act upon the world positively or negatively.[85] Human agency is the focus of chapter 2.

All respondents to Carr and co-author's interviews state that climate change should not be the church's top priority and some see it as detracting from the church's mission. However, some respondents believe that an environmental focus could complement the goal of evangelism.[86]

Finally, some respondents understand climate change through the lens of eschatology. Carr and co-authors found premillennial dispensationalist beliefs are antithetical to Evangelical environmentalism, as they emphasize the rapture of the faithful and the destruction of the Earth. Others apply the political prophecies in the book of Revelation to the rise of a one-world government, and hence they strongly oppose global greenhouse gas emissions regulation.[87] David Barker and David Bearce found that the belief in end times theology—by which they identify premillennial dispensationalism as the dominant belief in the United States—results in opposition to costly policies to deal with climate change. Such opposition is due to a shortening of the time horizon over which benefits can be weighed up against the economic costs involved.[88]

Millennialism and Capitalism

Early American postmillennialism informs American politics and its view of its own manifest destiny. As Michael Northcott observes,

---

85. Carr et al., "Faithful Skeptics," 291.
86. Carr et al., "Faithful Skeptics," 294–95.
87. Carr et al., "Faithful Skeptics," 292–93.
88. Barker and Bearce, "End-Times Theology," 267–79.

the reference "new world" to describe the Americas invokes the language of new heavens and new earth (Rev 21). Even political philosopher and agnostic Thomas Paine, who agitated for revolution against England, believed the new colony held the power to begin the world all over again.[89] Early American settlers believed they were building a godly commonwealth that would usher in the millennial rule of the saints.[90]

This view of the millennium began to give way to premillennialism after the American Civil War in the 1860s. Premillennialism is more pessimistic about human nature. Human history is in decline, headed towards the great tribulation which is marked by an increase in sin and wickedness, wars, and natural catastrophes. Climate change is simply one aspect of the great tribulation. From this time of suffering, "the faithful" are "saved" by being raptured from the Earth.[91] In such a schema it is not difficult to see why climate change can be ignored: Humans can neither stop it nor are they adversely affected by it. Northcott describes this premillennialism as totally separating the "kingdom of this world" from the "kingdom of God." The church, in this view, forms no part of the course of events on Earth, being called only to "save souls," hence the emphasis on evangelism that Carr and co-authors identified. Given that the tribulation is part of the divine timetable, to engage in justice making—in an attempt to better the state of the world—is to thwart the divine purpose and delay Christ's return.[92] Thus some premillennials describe peace activism and environmental protection as "heresy."[93]

Yet Northcott claims that both views of the millennium discussed support the view that "Americans are in some exceptional sense in charge of human history." Either way, they are the true redeemer nation.[94] This redemption is made manifest through

---

89. Northcott, *Angel Directs the Storm*, 9.
90. Northcott, *Angel Directs the Storm*, 15.
91. Northcott, *Angel Directs the Storm*, 44.
92. Northcott, *Angel Directs the Storm*, 58–59.
93. Northcott, *Angel Directs the Storm*, 67.
94. Northcott, *Angel Directs the Storm*, 15.

economic activity. Northcott judges American religion to be just as consumer driven as is the American economy. He identifies America as anti-centrist and voluntarist, which has produced one of the few advanced industrial societies where religion continues to thrive. Churchgoers are consumers of a product, and this consumer mentality has produced a marriage of sorts between free market and religious fundamentalism.[95] This marriage informs Francis Fukuyama's view that we have reached "the end of history" where the free market has triumphed and America is history's *telos*.[96]

Northcott's analysis is supported by William Connolly. Rather than always sharing the same religious and economic doctrines, Connolly sees affinities of identity and of sensibility between Evangelical Christianity and what he calls the "cowboy capitalism of media and the Republican party."[97] The resonance between cowboy capitalism and the Evangelical Right is the future of the Earth. As Connolly comments: "One party discounts the future of the earth to extend its economic entitlements now, the other to prepare for the day of judgment against nonbelievers."[98] Both are thoroughly Holocene systems of thought. For Evangelicalism, the Anthropocene is the divinely-appointed exit from the Holocene for human wickedness. For capitalism, the Anthropocene is at worst a stage that humanity must pass through in its exercise of agency on the path of endless growth.

While there is an established relationship between millennial theology and capitalism in the United States, there are fewer studies for the Australian church. Miriam Pepper and Rosemary Leonard examined the relationship between ecotheological beliefs, which included eschatological beliefs, and environmental attitudes and behaviors.[99] Their study employed two ecological belief scales. The "God in nature" scale concerns the presence of God in the

---

95. Northcott, *Angel Directs the Storm*, 19–20.
96. Fukuyama, "End of History," 3–18.
97. Connolly, "Evangelical-Capitalist Resonance Machine," 871.
98. Connolly, "Evangelical-Capitalist Resonance Machine," 876.
99. Pepper and Leonard, "How Ecotheological Beliefs Vary," 101–24.

other than human, whereas the "Dominion" scale reflects the right for humanity to rule over the rest of creation, which exists primarily for human use, together with a dualistic end times theology.[100] These two scales were based on the strength of agreement with three questions about theological belief, on a scale of 1 (strongly disagree) to 5 (strongly agree). Dominion theology was measured by the degree of affirmation of statements about human dominion, a utilitarian approach to nature, and millennial theology. God in nature belief was measured by agreement to statements about God's presence in nature, including nature as a source of religious experience. Pepper and Leonard found that Australian churchgoers were less affirming of Dominion theology (overall mean of 3.15 and standard deviation of 0.94) than the God in nature view (mean 4.38, standard deviation 0.59). Given the importance of millennialism in the United States, it is noteworthy that for Australian churchgoers, the statement "Natural disasters and human-caused environmental degradation are signs of the end times" has a mean of 2.85 and standard deviation of 1.16.[101] This implies millennialism is less strongly adhered to in the Australian context.[102]

God in nature views were held strongly by their adherents, whereas there was more variation in adherence to Dominion theology across church traditions. In particular, these views were held more closely by conservative church traditions—including Evangelical Protestants and Pentecostals—than mainline Protestants and Catholics.[103] The ecotheological beliefs outlined were found to affect environmental attitudes and behaviors, hence addressing the issues raised by Dominion theology in conservative Australian churches is important.[104]

---

100. Pepper and Leonard, "How Ecotheological Beliefs Vary," 107.

101. Pepper and Leonard, "How Ecotheological Beliefs Vary," 108.

102. Hence, Philip Almond's assertion that Australian Prime Minister Scott Morrison's climate inaction is informed by his Pentecostalism's eschatology is an unsubstantiated assertion. See Almond, "Five Aspects of Pentecostalism."

103. Pepper and Leonard, "How Ecotheological Beliefs Vary," 113.

104. Pepper and Leonard, "How Ecotheological Beliefs Vary," 113–14.

From Creation to Canaan

Research Questions

As we have seen, understanding human agency is central to understanding the Anthropocene. Underpinning the Anthropocene is both capitalism and, at least in the United States context, millennial theology. Both of these views subvert human agency in making this new era both desirable (as necessary progress of divinely mandated judgement) and, it is argued, unavoidable. Overcoming the tendencies of Evangelical theology that minimize or dismiss environmental engagement can be addressed in part by a thorough re-thinking of the scriptural sources shared by Christianity and Judaism, and to a lesser extent by Islam.

In what follows, I consider the shared Primeval History, particularly Genesis 1–3, and the Holiness Code of Leviticus 17–26. I inquire into what was Israel's responsibility for the land, and how was this shaped by their understanding of divine sovereignty, and the nature of the land itself. And I ask: how might an understanding of this responsibility impact on religious communities who acknowledge this text as Scripture?

In chapter 2, I examine Gen 1:1—2:3, exegeting the Hebrew text. Three themes emerge from such a consideration. First, central to this creation story is the Sabbath. An underlying heptadic (sevenfold) structure supports the Sabbath etiology of Gen 2:2–3. Secondly, Gen 1:1—2:3, together with the Priestly Flood narrative, forms a *chaoskampf* or struggle against the forces of chaos. God constrains the forces of chaos to bring about order for the flourishing of human and non-human species. Hence, the Sabbath is a celebration of this victory, and forms a later layer added to the original Priestly account by the Holiness School (H). This view is supported more clearly by preferring the Masoretic text over the Septuagint. The *chaoskampf* demonstrates how God involves the creation in this act of ordering.

I then consider how Sabbath and temple are integrated in the P material, particularly in the Book of Exodus. Here, creation and temple are associated with the so-called "completion formulae;" i.e., the Tabernacle is creation in miniature and the creation is the

Tabernacle in macrocosm. The sanctification of both is conducted in the liturgical performances associated with Sabbath activities.

Turning then to Leviticus, I show how the Sabbath is a liturgical marriage between agriculture, history, and religious practice. In Leviticus, H unites the themes of Sabbath and sanctuary from the creation narrative. Sabbath underlies Israel's liturgical calendar, including the weekly provision of bread for the temple. To keep the Sabbath was an imitative act of holiness, reminding the people of their covenant status and *Yhwh* to bring the promised seasonal rains, holding at bay the chaos of failed crops, wild beasts, and foreign invaders.

Finally, I show that the earth/land is an active participant in *Yhwh*'s work of maintaining order and of bringing chaos into judgement. In Genesis, the earth demonstrates agency in its own unfolding. In Leviticus, this agency is seen in the requirement for the land to keep its own Sabbath, and in its role of judgement of its human inhabitants by vomiting them out for covenant violations.

In chapter 3, I argue that the Garden story (Gen 2:5—3:24) presents the *adam* as a sacral king in a sanctuary garden. Care of the garden represents cultic responsibility, while also being attentive to the needs of the soil outside of the temple precincts. Life outside the Garden represents Israel's exile from the land, but an ongoing relationship with both God and land is possible. The whole of Genesis through Leviticus can be interpreted from this perspective, at least from the point of view of the Priestly editing that joins together the earlier traditions. These three books propose the conditions under which a return to Eden might still be possible. Leviticus connects the protological temple theology of Gen 1:1—2:3 and the Garden as sanctuary theology of Gen 2:5—3:24 in an "Edenization" of Canaan. Care for the land is an expression of Israelite holiness.

Chapter 4 concludes the present work with some hermeneutical implications for doing theology in the Anthropocene, noting some areas for possible future research.

2

Sabbath Keeping in H

Genesis 1 and the Problem of the Anthropocene

Genesis 1 and Anthropocentrism

As discussed in the previous chapter, much Christian thinking on the Anthropocene is often crippled by the theological assumptions of Evangelicalism, including inerrancy, human sinfulness, and divine sovereignty and human responsibility. Eschatological views are applied to dismiss human action, or even produce a theological marriage between forms of millennialism and Western capitalism. This has implications for a theology of human vocation. It either de-motivates human action with the belief that humans can and should do nothing to intervene in ecological destruction; or, worse still, it suggests believers should actively participate to accelerate the eschaton.

My key hermeneutical concern is to develop a theological framework for human vocation grounded in the creation accounts in the book of Genesis. The exegetical focus is then an interpretation of the divine commands to both the human and other-than-human creatures in the Genesis creation narratives.

Such an endeavour is not without its problems. Writing in the 1960s, Lynn White famously argued that anthropocentric readings of Gen 1:26–28 are directly responsible for the present environmental crisis, which we now call the Anthropocene.¹ He identifies modern science and technology as distinctively *Occidental*, beginning in the Middle Ages, and grounded in the medieval worldview of "man and nature." He argues that Christianity in its Western form is "the most anthropocentric religion the world has seen," telling a story of creation "explicitly for man's benefit and rule."² This human-centered story replaced various forms of animism, leaving no reason to protect nature.³ White concludes then that modern science is "an extrapolation of natural theology" and that modern technology is "at least partly to be explained as an Occidental, voluntarist realization of the Christian dogma of man's transcendence of, and rightful mastery over, nature."⁴

The extent to which this understanding is true is debated.⁵ What can be asserted with confidence, however, is that this understanding is prevalent in some Christian traditions today.⁶ Scholars

---

1. White, "Historical Roots," 1203–7. For a more recent exploration of this view, see Morton, *Being Ecological*.

2. White, "Historical Roots," 1204–5. Significantly, White does acknowledge earlier stages of human impact that pre-date the Western Christianity of the Middle Ages, such as the Pleistocene extinctions, or domination of the Nile Delta by irrigation. However, he places the major responsibility for the ecologic crisis on the Western church.

3. "Nature" is often seen as a problematic term. Timothy Morton sees the term as flattening out the non-human other and inhibited our ability to have filial relationships with. Morton, *Being Ecological*, 144–45. Fixing the problem of change is, for some, dependent on collapsing the difference between humanity and nature. See Alberro, "Humanity and Nature Are Not Separate." In this thesis, I will typically use the term "nature" to refer to the non-human when discussing science, or human responsibility in general. However, when exegeting the biblical texts, I will use the term "creation" to refer to the non-human. This is not to ignore that both, from the perspective of the authors of Genesis 1–2, are creations of God. It is precisely to establish that creation itself has rights and responsibilities before God, which are both similar and different than those demanded of Israel in the first instance, and as discussed briefly in chapter 4, the church.

4. White, "Historical Roots," 1206.

5. See, for example, McGrath, *Reenchantment of Nature*; Harrison, "Fill the Earth and Subdue It," 3–24; Irving-Stonebraker, "From Eden to Savagery and Civilization," 63–79.

6. For a utilitarian, anthropocentric approach to nature, see, for example, Whelan et al., *Cross and the Rain Forest*.

have suggested that the text of Gen 1:26–28 appears less amenable to ecological readings than is Gen 2:15. Theodore Hiebert draws the contrast between the presentation of humans as masters of the land who subdue it, with humans as the land's servant.[7] Norman Habel identifies Gen 1:26–28 as a so-called "grey" text. These are texts that have been used to "justify our domination, devaluation and destruction of the planet."[8] The problematic words are *radah* and *kabash*. The former is typically translated as "rule" while the latter is translated as "subdue," "dominate," or "bring into bondage."[9] Habel concludes that it is more Christian to abandon Gen 1:26–28 for the "green" text of Gen 2:15: "To follow the way of Christ, then, is to follow the mission of 'serving' Earth enunciated in Genesis 2, rather than dominating nature as expressed in Genesis 1."[10] Such a view is not without its critics, and context dictates how *radah* and *kabash* should be translated.[11]

One dubious possibility, as Ronald Simkin suggests, would be to stress that the Priestly (P) creation story of Genesis 1 is focussed on God's role in creation, while the non-P creation myth of Genesis 2–3 focusses primarily on the role of human agents as

---

7. Hiebert, *Yahwist's Landscape Nature and Religion in Early Israel*, 157. Davis, *Scripture, Culture, and Agriculture*, 29.

8. Habel, *Inconvenient Text*, xvii.

9. Habel, *Inconvenient Text*, 2–6. In Numbers, *kabash* is used in the context of the conquest of Canaan (Num 32:22, 29).

10. Habel, *Inconvenient Text*, 77.

11. Terrence Fretheim for example argues that "development" is a better rendering *kabash*: "This process [i.e., kabash] offers to the human being the task of intra-creational development, of bringing the world along to its fullest creational potential." Fretheim, "Book of Genesis," 346. Davis understands as simply meaning "taking possession" in an exilic context of a displaced people unable to farm their land. In a similar vein, Walter Brueggemann sees the command to subdue as one of encouragement, a promise of return to the fertile land. See Brueggemann, "Kerygma of the Priestly Writers," 107. As we shall see later, the setting of the H reworking of Genesis 1 suggests it is from the Persian period (or "post-exilic") rather than exilic, although the pre-Sabbath version of the Priestly creation story is likely earlier, and so the arguments above may still be valid.

collaborators or co-creators with God.[12] Hence, the latter text is more green than grey, a better guide for developing an ethic for the Anthropocene. While one can value one tradition more highly than the other, the two creation accounts are joined with the *toledot* formula ("generations") used throughout Genesis. At least from an editor's point of view, the constituent texts are therefore meant to be read side by side.[13] This suggests that we might expect both tensions and commonalities. I will argue that creation is able to participate in its unfolding. This participation includes both the human and non-human. This participation can either be order maintaining, or viz a viz the Anthropocene, chaos releasing.

The Priestly Authorship of Genesis 1

The Pentateuch has a long and complex history of composition and redaction.[14] The scope of the present chapter is limited to the Priestly (P) school and its concerns. The Priestly memory is of a story of creation to law-giving stretching from Genesis to Numbers, but many scholars find earlier layers of P, especially before the book of Numbers.[15] I follow the approach of Mark Brett in assuming a shared political imaginary that may be the work of more than one generation of scribes. This includes P in dialogue with older sources.[16] Of particular interest here and in the next chap-

---

12. Simkin, "Creation and Theodicy," 237–39. Simkin oversimplifies the theology of Genesis 1.

13. The *toledot* formula is translated as "these are the generations of," which is used throughout Genesis (e.g., 6:9; 10:1; 11:10). An editor has joined the Priestly account to the Garden story by applying this formula in Genesis 2:4a. Zevit, *What Really Happened in the Garden of Eden?*, 77–78; Ramantwana, "Humanity Not Pronounced Good," 425–44.

14. For a recent review, see Albertz, "Recent Discussion of the Formation of the Pentateuch/Hexateuch," 65–92.

15. The Deuteronomist and Priestly traditions may either be joined as Pentateuch or Hexateuch, but the scope of the present study is P and its use of non-P materials. For a discussion of the end of the earliest P text (Pg), see Römer, "Problem of the Hexateuch," 820–22.

16. Brett, *Locations of God*, 56–57.

ter is the potential division of P to include the Holiness School (H).[17] The bulk of H is found in the Holiness Code of Leviticus 17–26. Differences in scholarly opinion emerge when it comes to the relationship between P and H outside of the Holiness Code, but there are reasons to think that H-like theology has been introduced also into Genesis.[18] Here, I adopt the majority view that H post-dates P.[19] Central to the argument developed here is that Gen 1:1—2:3 represent an H reworking of an earlier P creation story within Genesis 1, and that H develops this theology further in the Holiness Code (Lev 19–26) and other H-like texts such as Exod 31:12–17. The major focus of this reworking is the emphasis placed on the Sabbath, and its relationship to the sanctuary cult.[20]

17. Wright, "Holiness in Leviticus and Beyond," 351–64.

18. Arnold argues that Genesis 1 has been redacted by H from P and non-P materials. He claims that H found Genesis 2 as inadequate as a basis for matters of Priestly interest, namely Sabbath, animal taxonomy and dietary laws, and festival timings. Genesis 2:1–3 prepares the way for the Sabbath prohibitions in Exod 31:12–17 and 35:2–3, which he also identifies as H. The text also contains the lexeme *qodesh*, which is central to H (Lev 17–26). It could be argued that Gen 2:1–3 is an H insertion into an earlier P text, but according to Arnold, Gen 1:1—2:3 is likely a unity due to its consistent emphasis on the Sabbath, emphasized by an underlying heptadic structure. Words such as "day," "good," "earth," and "God" are used in multiples of seven. See Arnold, "Genesis 1 as Holiness Preamble," 331–43. Instead, following David Carr, I will argue below for several amendations to an earlier P text to shape the creation account into a Sabbath etiology. See Carr, "Standing at the Edge," 17–41. Furthermore, Cynthia Edenburg argues—both on lexical similarities between Genesis 2–4 and Leviticus 26, and on the way in which scrolls are manufactured—that Genesis 2–4 was added at a late pre-P stage, or at least before Gen 1:1—2:4a. See Edenburg, "From Eden to Babylon," 155–67.

19. Israel Knohl argues against the view that the laws underlying H antedate P. The older theory was based on the suggestion that Israelite religion evolved from a popular religion to a cultic one invented during the exile, as Wellhausen and others assumed. H, with its interest in agriculture, is seen as an intermediate stage in this evolution. Knohl prefers to see two independent schools, with H postdating P. See Knohl, *Sanctuary of Silence*, 6. Jeffrey Stackert argues that the distributed nature of H insertions outside of the Holiness Code suggests H was never an independent compositional unit. Stackert, "Holiness Code and Writings," 392.

20. See especially Carr. Also, Rhyder, "Sabbath and Sanctuary Cult in the Holiness Legislation," 721–40.

Aim and Outline

The aim of this chapter is to establish that in the Priestly (P) tradition, specifically the Holiness School (H), the creation is described as an active partner with God in its own unfolding and ordering.[21] For Israel, this involves the participation in the temple cult and Sabbath keeping, both as expressions of holiness. For the earth/land, participation is described both in terms of the initial act of ordering, and an ongoing covenant relationship with *Yhwh* and Israel. This relationship involves land keeping, Sabbath keeping, and acting as an agent of chaos when Israel breaks the covenant. Establishing this partnership involves exegesis of P's creation story (Gen 1:1—2:3) as well as the Flood narrative (Gen 6–8), and the Holiness Code (Lev 18, 25–26).

Firstly, I demonstrate that the creation story is now a Sabbath etiology, climaxing with the declaration of sacred time in Gen 2:2–3. Underlying this narrative is a tight heptadic structure, which is clearly imposed over an earlier P creation account. Establishing this in turn relies on considering textual variations, showing that the Masoretic is to be preferred over the harmonizing text of the Septuagint.

Secondly, I show that the original underlying creation account, together with P's Flood narrative is best understood as a *chaoskampf* or combat myth. God's initial act of creation is viewed as an act of ordering and of subduing (or holding at bay) chaos. However, chaos lurks in the background, threatening to be unleashed by human evil (Gen 6:5–8). Two key ideas follow from this understanding of creation.

The first is that the ordering of the creation is not by simple fiat, but rather involves and is responsive to creation's own agency and involvement in this ordering. God makes room for creation to be itself and to participate in its own development. This prefigures that active role of the land in maintaining order in H.

---

21. For a systematic theological approach to God's "making way" for the other, see, for example, Moltmann, *Science and Wisdom*, 119–20.

The second key idea is that the defeat of chaos is also tied up in the enthronement of God. In contemporary myths, a deity would be enthroned in their temple after defeating opposing forces. Genesis 1:1—2:3 anticipates the completion of the Tabernacle in Exodus, and the divine presence. This theme is pursued further in chapter 3 where I examine Eden as temple sanctuary, and the Edenization of Canaan.

Finally, I demonstrate how H unites the themes of creation, Sabbath, and temple. Sabbath keeping mimetically re-enacts this ordering on a weekly basis.[22] It serves as a reminder to *Yhwh* of the covenant promises to maintain order by bringing seasonal rains and bountiful harvests. It also serves as a reminder to Israel of her calling to be holy in reverencing the temple and keeping the Sabbath.

I also briefly examine the requirement that the land also had to keep a Sabbath to *Yhwh*, and that Israel's interference with the land's obligation led to chaos in the form of exile. Remarkably, the land punishes the humans by vomiting out impurities.

The Sabbath in Genesis 1:1—2:3

Sabbath in Creation and the Heptadic Structure of Genesis 1:1—2:3

In this section, I argue that the climax of the Priestly creation account (Gen 1:1—2:3) is the Sabbath etiology of Gen 2:2-3.[23] However, a closer examination of the text by comparing the main textual variants, reveals that this Sabbath etiology is a later edition to an earlier Priestly creation account. The two main textual variation I consider here, following Ronald Hendel, are the Masoretic text (MT or M) and the Greek Septuagint (LXX or G) which has a proto-G Hebrew *Vorlage*.[24]

---

22. Levenson, *Creation and the Persistence of Evil*, 77.
23. Arnold, "Genesis 1 as Holiness Preamble," 334.
24. Hendel argues that we need to take G (the old Greek) seriously as a conservative translation of an underlying Hebrew variant, not merely a free

Establishing the secondary nature of the Sabbath achieves two things. Firstly, it enables a better understanding of the importance of the Sabbath in the text, and its development later in H. Secondly, identifying the underlying account allows an exploration of the relationship between the two. Sabbath keeping becomes a key to the unfolding of the Priestly traditions.

The centrality of the Sabbath is reinforced by the pattern of sevens, or heptadic structure. The obvious heptad is that of the seven *yom* ("days") of creation[25], but other key words include *erets* ("earth") used twenty-one times, and *Elohim* ("God") used thirty-five times.[26] On the first day (vv. 2–5), *or* ("light") is used five times, and its synonym *yom* (see Gen 1:5) twice. The phrase *wayhi ken* ("and it was so") occurs six times in M (vv. 7, 9, 11, 15, 24, 30). It is not found on day five but occurs twice on day six. This phrase forms a heptad with *wayhi or* ("and there was light") on the first day (v. 3). In G, *wayhi ken* is found in verse 6 instead of 7, but is also used on day five (v. 20) to form a heptad with *wayhi or*.

The typical structure of the creation story is a report on God's word, followed by *wayhi ken* and a report on God's deed. Verses 6–7 follow this structure in G, whereas *wayhi ken* is located at the end of verse 7 in M.[27] Two possibilities present themselves. The first is that G is original, and M is the result of a deliberate change or a scribal error. Hendel sees no obvious reason for either to be the case. The other possibility is that M is original, and G has produced a harmonization to produce a more "perfect" account. This is consistent with the observation that P is understood to offset repetition with small variations.[28] Hence, we apply the general principle that the more difficult reading is to be preferred.

---

rendering of M. This has been confirmed by comparison with documents from Qumran. Hendel, *Text of Genesis 1–11*, 17–18.

25. Levenson, *Creation and the Persistence of Evil*, 100.

26. Excluding 2:4a from P. On Gen 2:4a as an editorial join between P and the so-called Yahwist account, see Zevit, *What Really Happened in the Garden of Eden?*, 77–78.

27. Hendel, *Text of Genesis 1–11*, 21.

28. Hendel, *Text of Genesis 1–11*, 21.

Likewise, the extra *wayhi ken* in v. 20 is more likely an addition by G than a deliberate omission in M.²⁹ The heptadic structure of H therefore includes *wayhi or* as in M, rather than its exclusion for *wayhi ken* in v. 20. Clearly then, the seven-fold structure is important to the text, whether G's irregular structured text, or M's attempt to correct and further emphasise its importance.

Another heptadic phrase is *wayar Elohim ki tov* ("and God saw that it was good"). This phrase is found six times in M (vv. 4, 10, 12, 18, 21, 25), but is lacking on day two. The longer phrase *wayar Elohim . . . tov meod* ("and God saw . . . very good") in v. 31 completes the heptad in M. As was the case for *wayhi ken*, G includes the phrase where a "perfect" structure demands it. It is reasonable to assume that here as before, G is producing a harmonized text.

The last important textual variation is found Gen 2:2a, where M's use of *hashebii* ("the seventh [day]") is a difficult rendering, but in my view likely original. Hendel argues this reading is "manifestly incorrect" according to the narrative context, and follows G, S, Syr and Jub in the use of *hashishi* ("God ended his work on the sixth [day]").³⁰ The phrase *waycal* ("and were finished/ended") is repeated in vv. 1 and 2, with no apparent difference in grammatical usage. This creates tension between Gen 1:31 and 2:2a. In Gen 1:31, God evaluates the creation on the sixth day, which is then pronounced as finished (*waycal*) in Gen 2:1. In Gen 2:2a, God finished (*waycalu*) his work on *hashebii* ("the seventh [day]"). Reading G as original means that the *hashebii* in 2a is, according to Hendel, an "accidental assimilation by anticipation" of the similar phase in v 2b. There are three reasons for rejecting this view.

First, as we have seen previously, the usual pattern is that the easier reading of *hashishi* is more likely to be a correction of the original *hashebii*. Secondly, as Hendel himself suggests, G, S, and Syr likely derive from a common root.³¹ Hence, his preference rests on not multiple attestations against M, but one alternative

29. Hendel, *Text of Genesis 1–11*, 22.
30. Hendel, *Text of Genesis 1–11*, 32.
31. Hendel, *Text of Genesis 1–11*, 33.

tradition. Thirdly, following the observation of P's tendency to repeat phrases with small variations, vv. 2a, b, and 3 demonstrate parallels that suggest an unity for the purposes of stressing the seventh day:

> v. 2a "On the seventh day [*bayyom hashebii*] God finished the work that he had done [*melaktow asher asah*]."
>
> v. 2b "And he rested on the seventh day [*bayyom hashebii*] from all the work which he had done [*mikkal melaktow asher asah*]."
>
> v. 3 "the seventh day [*yom hashebii*] . . . in it God rested from all the work which he had created [*mikkal melaktow asher bara*]."

Hence, while *hashebii* is difficult in v. 2a, its parallels with vv. 2b–3 support the argument that vv. 2–3 are additions to an earlier text, along with the heptadic structure of the creation account.

Further arguments for the later addition of Sabbath theology are presented by David Carr.[32] Firstly, there is the striking divergence between eight creation acts and six days of creation. While there is symmetry with two acts of creation on days three and six, there are some strange splits, such as the separating and gathering of waters (days two and three) and the creation of light and lights (days one and four). Also problematic is the alternation of day and night from day one, before the sun and other lights were created on day four. This suggests that the six day structure was imposed on a pre-existing creation account.

It then follows that Gen 2:2–3 was a scribal key to the heptadic structure, and that it too is an addition. Genesis 1:1 and 2:1 form an inclusio with the creation of the heavens (*hashamayim*) and earth (*bereshit bara Elohim et hashamayim wahaarets*) were finished (*waykalu hashamayim wahaarets*). To this original inclusio was added the six days, including the overall evaluating statement on *kal asher asah* ("all that he had made") in 1:30. The repetition of *kalah* in Gen 2:2a from v. 1 indicates the introduction of a new idea, that of the Sabbath day. Parallels between the three

---

32. Carr, "Standing at the Edge,": 17–41; cf. Achenbach, "Sabbath," 18–32.

instances of *hashebii* have already been noted. God's initial work of creation and subduing chaos is not ultimately complete until God rests (*shabat*), blesses (*barek*) and sanctifies (*qadesh*) the seventh day. Note that God sanctifies the seventh day because (*ki*) in it God rested (*shabat*) from all the work of creation. The implication of v. 3 is that this work was completed on the seventh day. A new inclusio in Gen 2:3 is formed by repeating the phrase *bara Elohim* ("God created") from Gen 1:1. Genesis 2:2–3 therefore form a new conclusion to a seven-day pattern in Gen 1:1–2:3 that provides a rationale for Sabbath keeping later in H, based in God's own ceasing from labor.[33]

Carr suggests that Gen 1:3–5 is also an addition, while others like Thomas Krüger and Reinhard Achenbach, include these verses in their pre-Sabbath Priestly document.[34] Genesis 1:3a is unusually brief and does not give a purpose for the creation of light (cf. Gen 1:6, the dome; 14–15, the lights in the dome).[35] Further, there are variations in two phrases in v. 3. In v. 3b, the execution formula of *wayhi ken* is replaced by *wayhi or*. Likewise, in v. 3a the phrase *wayyar Elohim ki tov* ("and God saw that it was good") is replaced by *wayyar Elohim et haor tov* ("and God saw that the light was good"). These irregularities point to Gen 1:3–5 as an addition to stress the importance of light. The purpose of the light is not explicitly mentioned in v. 3 but is explained in vv. 4–5 as defining day by its separation from the pre-existent darkness. Since we have argued that the days of creation are an addition, it likely follows that the creation of light to mark those days is also an addition.[36] Whatever we might conclude about the nuances of editorial history, these reflections serve to highlight the importance of the Sabbath in the text, and direct our attention to its development in H.

---

33. The fact that the Sabbath is not taken up again in P, but is clearly developed in H texts, it is more likely that the MT should be followed. See Krüger, "Genesis 1:1—2:3," 130–31.

34. Krüger, "Genesis 1:1—2:3," 134. Achenbach, "Sabbath," 23.

35. Carr further adds 1:9a, but nothing is created, only separated.

36. Carr, *Standing at the Edge*, 23.

Sabbath and *Chaoskampf*: The Struggle against Chaos

Having identified that the Sabbath is central to H's reworking of the original P creation story, I now turn to P's account. The goal is not to reconstruct this account precisely but examine P's version of the *chaoskampf* or combat myth. Given the somewhat controversial nature of this hypothesis, I will need to spend some time defending the view by also considering P's Flood account. I then bring these two themes, *chaoskampf* and Sabbath together.

Jon Levenson understands the essence of the idea of creation in the Hebrew Bible as the constraining of the forces of disorder.[37] He argues that Genesis 1 represents a late stage in the development of Hebrew creation theology. Although muted, an underlying combat myth—still evident in other texts within the Hebrew Bible—is transformed to show that God constrains chaos to create order. While divine control is never relinquished, it is "often agonizingly, catastrophically dormant." This means that God leaves room for creation, including human responsibility, to play a role in the maintaining of order over chaos. Levenson then argues that divine omnipotence as *in potentia* is not the exercise of raw power, but of working with creation. The human rest on the Sabbath arguably continues this theme, as ceaseless labor is neither trusting of divine providence through creation, nor working with creation by allowing it to keep its Sabbath. I return to this theme when considering Leviticus 25–26.

Similarities between Genesis 1, Psalm 104, and the Babylonian creation myth *Enuma Elish* have long been noted.[38] In *Enuma Elish*, the god Marduk gains ascendency in the Babylonian pantheon by slaying the sea monster Tiamat and making the heavens

---

37. Levenson argues that the Hebrew Bible points to the "uncompromized mastery of YHWH." Genesis 1 does not present a theogony. However, neither does the text support creation *ex nihilo*. There is a plurality of creation texts that precede Genesis 1 and lie behind it, that support creation as a defeat of the forces of disorder. Levenson, *Creation and the Persistence of Evil*, 3–13.

38. The story dates to the second millennium BCE, with a Sumerian antecedent dating back a millennium earlier. Enns, *Evolution of Adam*, 38. See also Heidel, *Babylonian Genesis*, 12.

and land by dividing her corpse. Elements of the ascendency narrative are retained in Psalm 82 but are often obscured by English translations. The New American Standard Bible (NASB) translates v. 1 *"Elohim* takes his stand in the assembly of *El"* as "God takes his stand in his own congregation."[39] Verses 6–7 read, in the NASB translation:

> I said, "You are gods [*Elohim*], and all of you are sons of the Most High [*Elyon*]. Nevertheless you will die like men [*kiadam*], and fall like any one of the princes." Arise, O God [*Elohim*], judge the earth! For it is You who possesses all the nations.

The multiple uses of *Elohim* are obscured by translating one as singular and the other as plural. The New International Version places "gods" in quotation marks to indicate it is not to be read literally as divine figures, but rather as a parallelism for human princes. However, if the second use of *Elohim* is taken to refer to lesser deities, and *Elohim* is a separate god to *El* and *Elyon*, then the comparison with the *Enuma Elish* becomes obvious.

Psalm 74 documents the theme of creation by divine combat. Verses 12–17 echo the storm god Baal's defeat of the sea (*yam*).[40] There are shared themes with Genesis 1; i.e., the identification of day and night and the creation of light and the sun (v. 16; cf. Gen 1:2–5, 14–16), the boundaries of the earth (v. 17a; cf. Gen 1:9–10), and the creation of seasons (v. 17b; cf. Gen 1:14). The combat is described explicitly in verses 13–14:

> You divided the sea [*yam*] by your might; You broke the heads of the dragons [*tanninim*] in the waters. You crushed the heads of Leviathan [*liwyatan*]; you gave him as food for the creatures of the wilderness.

The *yam* is divided just as Marduk divided the corpse of Tiamat to form heaven and earth. By implication, *Elohim's* victory over the chaos's monsters is an act of creation, but a non-violent one

---

39. The text potentially implies an underlying henotheism. For a review, see Heiser, "Monotheism," 1–30.

40. Levenson, *Creation and the Persistence of Evil*, 7–9.

in this case. Elsewhere, we learn that the chaos monster survives, albeit under bounds. In Job 38:8–11, the proud *yam* is shut in with doors and bars. In Ps 104:6–9, the earth is covered in the *tehom* (cf. Gen 1:2). The waters flee *Yhwh*'s rebuke and may not pass over their boundary. In verse 26, Leviathan is formed for *Yhwh*'s amusement.[41]

The account in Genesis 1 is demythologized, with the combat myth reduced to "creation without opposition."[42] The dragon Tiamat becomes the depersonalized deep or *tehom* (v. 2).[43] Likewise, in Gen 1:6, the waters are separated. The great *tanninim* are not the children of Tiamat but are merely created beings.[44] That they are named explicitly is significant. A polemical statement is being made: God's power extends over the "gods" of Babylon and has chaos firmly under control. With the inclusion of the Sabbath etiology of Gen 2:2–3, Levenson argues that Marduk's divine ascendency is eclipsed by that of *Elohim*. God ceases or rests from the act of creation.[45] Konrad Schmidt argues that the P's use of *Elohim* is particularly significant.[46] The "Priestly usage of *Elohim* as a proper noun is programmatic in terms of an *inclusive monotheism*." This is because *Elohim* is a noun that can be translated as "gods," but wherever it is used in P it is always construed as singular, and hence, all other "gods" are "included in this notion of God."[47]

---

41. Levenson describing it as Yhwh's "rubber ducky." Levenson, *Creation and the Persistence of Evil*, 17. For a different take on the importance of chaos and its rehabilitation as a maternal image, see Keller, *Face of the Deep*; Artson, "Vibrating over the Face of the Deep," 40–47.

42. Levenson, *Creation and the Persistence of Evil*, 122.

43. Levenson, *Creation and the Persistence of Evil*, 55.

44. Mobley, *Return of the Chaos Monsters*, 20.

45. The completion formula of Gen 2:1–3 is mirrored in that of the Tabernacle (Exod 39:32, 43; 40:9–11, 33b–34). Creation can be pictured as the prototypical Tabernacle, and the Tabernacle as the creation in miniature. See Levenson, *Creation and the Persistence of Evil*, 85.

46. Schmid, "Quest for 'God,'" 271–89.

47. Schmid, "Quest for 'God,'" 285.

Carr argues against a parallel between *Enuma Elish* and and Gen 1:3–5 and 2:2–3, since these form part of the later Sabbath layer.[48] While a case can be made, as Levenson does for Gen 2:2–3, by contrast, Gen 1:3–5 do not find parallels in either *Enuma Elish*, or Psalm 104. In *Enuma Elish*, the day-night structure is assumed; Marduk is not reported to have created it. Likewise, in Psalm 104 light is what *Yhwh* wears as a garment (v. 2). As noted earlier, in Gen 1:3, light results from divine speech (*wayomer Elohim*).

How then does this muted combat myth in Genesis 1 demonstrate that divine sovereignty is *in potentia*? Levenson observes that the combat myth is evoked in times of national crisis with a call for God to reassert divine mastery. For example, Psalm 74 begins with the cry "O God, why have you rejected us forever?" (v. 1). The recounting of *Yhwh*'s primeval ordering of chaos in vv. 12–17 is bookended by the present plight of Israel:[49]

> v. 10–11: The enemy mocks and reviles the divine name while God withholds his [saving] right hand.

> vv. 12–17: God works salvation, dividing the sea [*yam*], conquering sea monsters [*tanninim*] and Leviathan [*liwyatan*], and imposing order on creation.

> vv. 18–20: The enemy mocks and reviles the divine name; *Yhwh* is called upon to save his people and remember the covenant.[50]

Yhwh has allowed Israel time to experience divine anger for covenant violation (v. 1). Psalm 74 is therefore an attempt to rouse *Yhwh* to remember his people and the covenant he made with them (vv. 2, 20), and to destroy his enemies (v. 11). At first glance, this might appear to reduce Israel's responsibility to a passive role

---

48. Carr, *Standing at the Edge*, 31.

49. Levenson, *Creation and the Persistence of Evil*, 11.

50. When quoting scriptural passages, I have used the transliteration *Yhwh* instead of the usual translation "Lord." This is to help distinguish the various biblical sources and the theological significance of the different names for God."

of invoking divine mercy. However, the combat myth provides the framework for a broader participation I will discuss later.

In Defense of the *Chaoskampf* in Genesis 1

Not all scholars are convinced that the *Chaoskampf* underlies the creation myth of Genesis 1. David Tsumura argues against an etymological connection between *tehom* (deep) and Tiamat.[51] Richard Averbeck further notes that the *tehom* (Gen 1:2) and *tanninim* (sea monsters, Gen 1:21) offer no challenge to God.[52] However, as Levenson observes, *tanninim* is used to refer to Leviathan (Is 27:1).[53] Perhaps Bernard Batto's less dogmatic observation circumvents any etymological issues in asserting that "P's world view was grounded in the cultural idiom of a common Semitic Combat Myth."[54]

One issue with the *Chaoskampf* interpretation is the meaning of *choshek* (darkness). Averbeck argues that *choshek* is good because it forms part of the alternating of darkness and light in the day/night sequence, which is the backbone of a creative structure that is pronounced very good (Gen 1:31). However, this neglects the fact that the heptadic structure of *tov* is a later Sabbath layer on an earlier P creation myth. The darkness appears to be part of the formlessness of the earth where "the earth was formless and void and darkness was over the face of the deep" (*wehaarets hayetah tohu wabohu wahoshek al pene tehom*, v. 2). Only the light is proclaimed good because it is clearly a creation of God (vv. 3–5). The darkness may not be evil, but it at least represents the chaotic. It was waiting for ordering into a pattern for time, culminating in the divine rest, the basis for human Sabbath keeping.

Another problem with critiques of the *Chaoskampf* interpretation in Genesis 1, is reading it in isolation from P's larger

---

51. Tsumura, *Creation and Destruction*, 36–57.
52. Averbeck, "Three 'Daughters' of Ba'al," 249.
53. Levenson, *Creation and the Persistence of Evil*, 54.
54. Batto, "Image of God in the Priestly Creation Account," 169.

Primeval narrative (Gen 1–9), which includes the Flood.[55] The Flood story in P begins with Noah, who is found to be righteous and blameless (Gen 6:9–10). The state of the *erets* is described in vv. 11–12 in two parallel statements. In vv. 11a, 12a, the *erets* is proclaimed *shachath* ("corrupt"). Verse 11a is a declaration that the *erets* is corrupt *lipne Elohim* (lit. "before God's face"). God then investigates the situation in v. 12a with an evaluative *wayar* ("and he saw"). Instead of finding the *erets* as *tov* (cf. Gen 1:4, 10, 12, 18, 21, 25) it is *shachath*. In particular, the use of *wehinneh* ("and indeed") in Gen 6:12a recalls the summative evaluation of Genesis 1:25. Just as *kal* ("all") was declared *tov* so now the *erets* is a circumlocution for all God has made and is found to be *shachath*. The reason for this corruption is given in v12b, *ki* ("for") *kal basar* ("all flesh") have corrupted their way on the *erets*. In parallel to v11b, this corruption of *kal basar* is the filling of the *erets* with *hamas* ("violence").

The Flood is the resurgence of the deep, as the *mayenoth tehom* ("fountains of the deep") burst forth to cover the earth (Gen 7:11; 8:2; cf. 1:2). Batto describes this as the deep breaking out of its prison to challenge the sovereign God's will. However, it is the divine decision to destroy the *erets* and *kal basar* (Gen 6:13). After the floodwaters had subsided, God set his *kesheth* ("bow") in the sky as a reminder to himself of the covenant between him and all of creation that the waters would never again become a flood to destroy all of creation (Gen 9:15). This parallels the account in the *Enuma Elish*, where Marduk "hangs up" his *kesheth* after defeating the last of his enemies.[56] So does the hanging of the bow in the sky in Genesis mean an end of hostilities between God and all flesh, or God and the deep? The emphasis in Genesis 7 and 8 is the bursting forth, rather than a divine releasing. In Gen 1:2, a divine wind *ruach Elohim* (divine wind or breath) blew over the *tehom* to bring order. In Gen 8:2, God makes a *ruach* to pass over the earth that stops the *mayenoth tehom*. Batto sees echoes of Baal, the storm god who brings a powerful wind and rides the clouds. Although the

---

55. Batto, "Image of God in the Priestly Creation Account," 169.
56. Batto, "Image of God in the Priestly Creation Account," 170.

deep is released to bring judgment on the violence on the earth, nonetheless the victory over the deep is a recapitulation of that at creation. As per contemporary Near Eastern myths, divine victory is followed by temple building.[57]

Sabbath and Temple

The building of the Jerusalem temple is prefigured rather than explicit in Gen 1:1—2:3. As in the case of the Sabbath, Gen 1:1—2:3 does not establish creation as a temple directly, but rather establishes an etiology for the construction of the Tabernacle. There are three parallels between the Priestly creation account and the completion of the Tabernacle in the so-called completion formula.

> Gen 2:2a: *waykal Elohim . . . melaktow* ("And God completed . . . his work"). // Exod 39:32a *watekel kal abodat* ("And finished all the work").

> Gen 1:31a: *wayar Elohim et kal asher asah wehinneh* ("And God saw all that he had made and indeed"). // Exod 39:43a *wayah Moses et kal hamelakah wehinneh* ("And Moses saw all the work and indeed").

> Gen 2:2a // Exod 40:33b: *waykal Moses asher et hamelakah* ("And Moses completed all the work").

Other lexical similarities include *barak* ("blessing") (Gen 2:3 of the seventh day // Exod 39:43 the sons of Israel), and sanctifying (Gen 2:3 *weyqadseh*, the seventh day // Exod 40:9 *weqidashta*, the Tabernacle).

A connection between Tabernacle to the Sabbath is also seen by comparing Exod 24:15–16 with Exodus 40 and Leviticus 1.[58] At the completion of the Tabernacle (Exod 40:33b), the glory of *Yhwh* fills it (*ukebod Yhwh male et hamishkan*, Exod 40:34). The cloud covers the mountain (Exod 24:15) and the Tabernacle (Exod 40:34) with the glory of *Yhwh* (*kebod Yhwh*). The LORD calls to

---

57. Batto, "Image of God in the Priestly Creation Account," 171–72.
58. See Weinfeld, "Sabbath, Temple, and the Enthronement of the Lord," 504.

Moses (*wayyiqra el Moses*) from the cloud and the Tabernacle (Exod 24:16 // Lev 1:1), in the former case on the seventh day, to receive instructions on how to build the Tabernacle (Exod 25:9).

The completion formula are therefore likely later additions to P, linking P's creation narrative to the creation of the Tabernacle. Therefore, as Levenson observes, the Tabernacle may be understood as creation in miniature, while creation is the Tabernacle on the macroscale, albeit underdeveloped in Gen 1:1—2:3. The heptadic structure reflects and replaces the equinox New Year festivals, as both Tabernacles (vernal equinox) and Passover (autumnal equinox) are seven days long. This shift, according to Levenson, means that creation is completed, consummated, and mimetically re-enacted in the Sabbath. Hence Sabbath keeping is one way that order is maintained against the forces of chaos.[59] Precisely how this occurs is discussed below.

Order, Agriculture, Festivals, and Sabbath

The ordering of chaos in Genesis 1 also has agricultural associations. The creation narrative ends with the provision of food for humans, livestock, animals of the field, and birds (vv. 29–30). It is possible, perhaps against expectations, that the watery chaos of Gen 1:2 (*tohu wabohu*) also has agricultural associations, as John Walton suggests.[60] The words *tohu* and *bohu* are, for example, found together in Isaiah 34. In this context, the rulers of Edom are judged for their hostility to Israel and the land is consequently destroyed:

> 11a the land will be occupied by wild animals
> 11b the land becomes desolate [*tohu*] and empty [*bohu*], unfit for agriculture
> 12 human rulers will be nothing
> 13a the land will be full of weeds, signs of agricultural collapse
> 13b–17 the land will be occupied by wild animals.

---

59. See Levenson, *Creation and the Persistence of Evil*, 76–77.
60. See Walton, *Lost World of Genesis One*, 49.

The NRSV translates v. 11b as "He shall stretch the line of confusion [*tohu*] over it, and the plummet of chaos [*bohu*] over its nobles," while the NASB reads: "And He will stretch over it the line of desolation [*tohu*] and the plumb line of emptiness [*bohu*]." The chiastic structure demonstrates that it is the land and not the rulers who become *tohu wabohu*. A related example is found in Jer 4:23, where the land of Judah becomes *tohu* and *bohu*, the fruitful fields a wilderness (v. 26) and the land devastated (v. 20). All of this was due to judgment on Israel's idolatry and injustices (Jer 4:1–2; cf. Hos 4:3).

Hence, following Walton's functional interpretation, Genesis 1 represents the imposition of agricultural order on the *tohu wabohu* over six days. Time is created on day one by the creation of light and its separation from darkness. This anticipates the creation of the lights to include the liturgical wording "seasons," including agricultural festivals, on day four. Space is created on day two, by the separation of the waters above from the waters below by the firmament. On the third day, food is created by separating the waters into one place and the dry ground in another where vegetation can grow.[61] Interestingly, the provision of plants for animal consumption in Gen 1:29–30 points beyond the human ordering of agriculture.[62] Instead, we see divine providential care for all creatures, and that human agricultural activity has appropriate bounds, seen also in the blessing to be fruitful and multiply to both humans and non-humans (Gen 1:28; cf. v. 22).

---

61. Walton, *Lost World of Genesis One*, 26.

62. Davis notes the key role that seeds play in this passage, highlighting agriculture as a key theme. From the earth comes forth sprout—out sprouts, plants seeding seed, and fruit trees bearing fruit. This self-perpetuation is consonant with the observations of Welker and Fretheim that the land participates in creation. The extended description points towards the particularity of place and the genetic diversity of Palestine, being one of the regions where agriculture began. Hence Davis concludes that the Priestly account is not too different from "the overtly agrarian character of the Yahwist's 'drama of soil.'" Davis, *Scripture, Culture, and Agriculture*, 50. On the origins of agriculture in the Levant, see Diamond, *Guns, Germs, and Steel*.

From Creation to Canaan

Michael LeFebvre makes an important connection between the lights on day four and the link between agriculture and the Hebrew festival calendar.[63] Genesis 1:14 reads:

> And God said, "Let there be lights in the dome of the sky to separate the day [*yom*] from the night [*halayelah*]; and let them be for signs [*leotot*] and for seasons [*ulemoadim*] and for days and years."

The word *moadim* is typically translated as "seasons," a climatological reference. LeFebvre instead argues that "festivals" or "feasts" is a preferred translation.[64] In Leviticus 23, the feasts of *Yhwh* (*moadi Yhwh*, v. 2) include the Sabbath and the seven annual feasts of Passover, Festival of Unleavened Bread, First Fruits, Festival of Weeks (Pentecost), Festival of Trumpets, Day of Atonement, and Tabernacles. Each of these feasts occurs in either spring or autumn and is tied to agricultural activity.[65] In this respect, Genesis 1 points to agricultural festivals.[66]

On day six, the living creatures (*nephesh chayah*) and humans are created, and as already mentioned, they share a vegetarian diet. The list of *nephesh chayah* includes livestock (*behemah*), creeping things (*remes*), and beasts of the field (*chatow erets*). The taxonomy of Gen 1:20–25 is used in Leviticus 11 to establish clean and unclean animals. LeFebvre suggests that therefore vv. 20–25 presents a taxonomy of farming.[67] More precisely the establishment of clean and unclean animals limits human meat consumption.[68] As humans were given green plants to eat at creation (Gen 1:29), and then everything after the flood (Gen 9:2–4), so H places limits on this (Lev 11:46–47).

The Sabbath is then a liturgical marriage between agriculture, history, and religious practice. Fretheim gives full expression to

---

63. LeFebvre, *Liturgy of Creation*, 14.
64. LeFebvre, *Liturgy of Creation*, 15.
65. LeFebvre, *Liturgy of Creation*, 39.
66. LeFebvre, *Liturgy of Creation*, 6.
67. LeFebvre, *Liturgy of Creation*, 173.
68. See Davis, *Scripture, Culture, and Agriculture*, 94–97.

Levenson's *in potentia* divine sovereignty when he observes that the divine Sabbath represents "giving time and space over to the creatures to be what they were created to be." God "sits back," creating creatures with "no strings attached." Israel, through faithful worship of God, becomes "attuned to a temporal order built into the very structure of creation."[69]

This liturgical marriage points to Genesis 1 as a text to order the whole life of Israel. It reminds the people that it is God who defeats the forces of chaos and provides for their needs. This God is the proper object of their worship. Human participation in the ongoing order of creation was to engage in worship in all aspects of life, particularly through the keeping of the seven annual festivals and the Sabbath.

This close association of "salvation history" with agricultural provision reminds us that dualist readings of New Testament eschatology are neither faithful to their Hebrew roots, let alone the texts themselves, nor equip the church for ethical reflection in the Anthropocene. For the Christian as for the Hebrews, salvation is intimately tied up with creation, a theme I will return to in the last chapter.

Sabbath Obedience in H

Sabbath and the Temple

Having now seen the importance of both Sabbath and temple in the Priestly creation story, I now turn to their development in H. Sabbath is discussed in the Holiness Code (Lev 17–26), and in what Julia Rhyder calls H-like texts, which share linguistic and thematic parallels with H. Rhyder argues that H originates in the Persian period, because it assumes the presence of the temple at key points. The purpose of H is therefore to ensure the success of the second temple cult.[70] However, while the assumed presence of the temple likely excludes an exilic provenance of H, this is also

---

69. Fretheim, *God and World*, 59.
70. Rhyder, "Sabbath and Sanctuary Cult," 721.

consistent with a pre-exilic provenance.[71] Choosing between pre- and post-exilic options does not affect the discussion that follows.

As noted earlier, the Sabbath etiology of Gen 2:2–3 is central to understanding the structure and purpose of the Priestly creation account. There is no explicit command at this point for humans to keep the Sabbath. However, God sanctifies (*kadesh*) the seventh day, creating holy or sanctified time, thus laying the foundation for Sabbath observance. In H, Sabbath keeping is for Israel the imitation of divine holiness, where Lev 19 vv. 2b and 3 form parallel statements:

> 2b: You shall be holy [*qidoshim tihyu*] for I *Yhwh* your God am holy [*ki qadosh ani Yhwh Elohim*].
>
> 3: Everyone of you shall revere his mother and his father and keep my Sabbaths, I am *Yhwh* your God [*ani Yhwh Elohim*].

Verse 2b introduces holiness as an imitative act, Israel shall be holy (*qidoshim*) because (*ki*) God is holy (*qadosh*). The use of God's covenant name *Yhwh* means that the imitative follows from their covenant relationship to *Yhwh*. Verse 3a explains v. 2b; i.e., Israel is holy by reverencing parents and keeping the Sabbath. Note in both the Deuteronomist and non-P giving of the ten commandments, honouring father and mother follows the commandment to keep the Sabbath (Exod 20:8–12; Deut 5:12–16). It is linked to long life in the land. In Lev 19:30, Sabbath keeping is linked with revering the sanctuary (*umiqadeshi tirau*). This commandment is repeated in Lev 26:2, and hence frames the commands in chapters 19–25.

The importance of Sabbath to H is shown in the festal calendar of Leviticus 23, as noted earlier. This chapter opens with a command for a total cessation of work on the Sabbath (*shabat shabaton*) (Lev 23:3; cf. Exod 31:15). The Sabbath is associated with a seven-day period and is used to calculate the time between First Fruits and Weeks (Lev 23:15–16). Total cessation (*shabat shabaton*) is also associated with Passover, the Day of Atonement, and

---

71. For a review of opinions on Leviticus as pre-monarchical, pre-exilic, exilic, and post-exilic, see Harper, "*I Will Walk among You*," 88–97.

Booths (Lev 23:5, 31–32, 39–43). Outside of the annual festivals, *shabat shabaton* is used to describe the seventh-year rest for the land, where no agricultural activities are permitted (Lev 25:2–7).

Rhyder acknowledges the consensus around Lev 25:2–7 as core H but notes a diversity of views on Leviticus 23. Verse 3 is generally recognized as late, as well as vv. 39–43. Verses 37–38 note that the Sabbath must be honoured besides the appointed times of *Yhwh* (*moadi Yhwh*); i.e., it is not included in them. However, the repeated use of *shabat* and *shabat shabaton* to calculate the timing of the festivals indicates that Sabbath is not secondary in the body of the calendar (15b–16, 24, 32). Rhyder shows that cessation of labor (*shabat shabaton*) is also emphasized in the H-like passages of Exod 31:12–17, and 35:1–3.[72] Leviticus 23:3 is repeated almost verbatim in Exod 35:2:

> Lev 23:3: Six days shall work be done; but the seventh day is a sabbath of complete rest [*shabat shabaton*], a holy convocation; you shall do no work: it is a sabbath [*shabat*] to *Yhwh*.
>
> Exod 35:2: Six days shall work be done, but on the seventh day you shall have a holy sabbath of solemn rest [*shabat shabaton*] to *Yhwh*.

Exodus 31:12–17 contains typical H phrasing, for example "you shall keep my Sabbaths" (*et shabettotay tishmoru*, Exod 31:13; cf. Lev 19:3, 30; 26:2) and "I am *Yhwh* who sanctifies you" (Exod 31:13; cf. Lev 20:8; 21:8; 26:2). The reminder that *Yhwh* is the one who sanctifies his people echoes the sanctification of the seventh day. The total cessation of work then reminds Israel of how *Yhwh* can order chaos to create holy time and space. Based on these similarities, Sabbath keeping in Exod 31:12–17 is also imitative.[73]

---

72. Rhyder, "Sabbath and Sanctuary Cult," 726–27.

73. Jeffrey Stackert argues unconvincingly that Sabbath obedience in Exod 31:12–17 is not imitative. Briefly, his argument hinges on the meaning of *ki* in the phrase *oth hi leolam ki* ("it is a sign forever for/that," v. 17). If *ki* is rendered as "that," Sabbath keeping is best understood as a reminder. If *ki* is rendered as "for," then Sabbath observance is imitative. Stackert provides three examples the construction of *ki* following *oth* ("sign") implies *ki* is "that." However, none

Levenson asserts that Sabbath keeping maintains order against the forces of chaos.[74] How then does this function? Sabbath keeping is imitative in two aspects, both of which reflect Israel's call to be holy. The second of these reflects Israel's imitative holiness with respect to its covenant responsibility to the land, considered in the next section. The first, discussed here, is Sabbath keeping as a covenant sign to *Yhwh*.

Covenant signs (*oth*) are for both partners. In Exod 12:13, the sign is clearly for both *Yhwh and* Israel. When *Yhwh* sees the blood on the lintel, he passes over the house without judgment. The blood is also a "sign for you" (*lekem leoth*), i.e., one of reassurance. In Genesis 9:12–17, the rainbow is a *leoth berith* ("sign of the covenant") which is *beni uben kal basar* ("between me and all flesh," v. 17). The sign is for God to remember the covenant and never again flood the earth (vv. 15–16). However, since it is God who brings the clouds over the sky that the bow is associated with (v. 14), the bow also acts to remind Israel.

In Exod 31:17, the Sabbath *beni uben bene yisrael oth hi leolam* ("it is a sign forever between me *and* the people of Israel"). As we have seen, Sabbath keeping is imititative of *Yhwh*'s holiness and therefore a sign to the people that they are holy. Levenson also argues that the close connection of Sabbath and new year festivals means that Sabbath obedience is a call to *Yhwh* to provide enough rainfall during the winter months for the spring harvest.[75] The chaos of winter needs divine control once more. In H, there is a clear link between obedience to the commandments and the seasonal rain (Lev 26:3–4). Hence, the people participate in the maintenance of order insofar as in H's cosmology, regular rains are dependent upon the divine blessing of covenant obedience.

---

of these examples are from P or H. The first two examples are from Exodus (3:12; 13:11–16) are identified by Thomas Dozeman as non-P, while Stackert's third example is from 2 Kgs 20:8–9. There is no immediate argument to draw to insist that *ki* cannot be imitative. Stackert, "Compositional Strata in the Priestly Sabbath,"; Dozeman, *Exodus*, 94–111.

74. Levenson, *Creation and the Persistence of Evil*, 76–77.
75. Levenson, *Creation and the Persistence of Evil*, 77.

While the Priestly Leviticus (chapters 1–16) is concerned with the activities of the priests and temple, Sabbath observance is clearly for the people in H. However, the temple association with Sabbath is reinforced in Lev 24:4–9. On the Sabbath Aaron was to replenish the loaves on the golden table of the inner sanctum. The phrase from the second half of v. 8 is somewhat enigmatic, *tamid meet bene Yisrael berith olam* ("continually from the sons of Israel by an everlasting covenant"). Rhyder takes this to mean that the people were responsible for providing the grain so that the bread could be replaced weekly. Further, she notes that the Sabbath is mentioned in connection with the fixed times of *Yhwh* (*moadi Yhwh*) in Lev 23:37–38 which involve food offerings. This implies that in this context, Sabbaths of *Yhwh* is a circumlocution for Sabbath sacrifices.[76] Thus, the two-fold requirement of the Sabbath to "keep my Sabbaths and revere my sanctuary" (Lev 19:30) is connected to the cosmic victory over chaos in Genesis 1. Holy human participation entails both the cessation of labor and cultic celebration of creation (made explicit in Exod 20:11).

Sabbath and the Land

My final consideration is the mutual obligation that the people and the land have to observe the Sabbath. Before examining the relevant texts in Leviticus 25–26, it is important to note the active role creation plays in the creation story. Creation is seen by Levenson as a drama, with real actors, both human and non-human.[77] In particular, the *erets* which is initially formless and void is declared good at each stage of its ordering. God names what he creates (Gen 1:5a, 8a, 10a) and separates what already exists (Gen 1:4b, 7b). He engages with creation as an active (covenant) partner. As Terrence Fretheim observes, divine creating entails a "speaking *with* that which is *already* created." The Priestly author uses a jussive "let,"

---

76. Rhyder, "Sabbath and Sanctuary Cult," 728–30.

77. Such an understanding is implicit in Levenson's subtitle, *Jewish Drama of Divine Omnipotence.*

leaving room for creaturely response.[78] This is evident in the fruitfulness of the *erets* as it brought forth (*watowtse*) vegetation (v. 12) in response to the command to do so (*tadshe*, v. 11), and the living creatures apart from humans (vv. 24–25). Such bringing forth is also used to describe Ruth's bringing out to Naomi the results of her gleaning (Ruth 2:18), and God bringing Israel out of Egypt (Jer 32:21).

This approach emphasizes what Michael Welker describes as the "*connectedness and cooperation* of creator and that which is creaturely."[79] This understanding of creation cooperating with the creator with its own sense of agency has been resisted by many exegetes, although it has long-standing support in the theological tradition. As Mari Joerstad correctly observes, any resistance to the creation's participation comes from the dualistic assumption that creation must either be divinized or inanimate.[80] The former assumption is avoided by Christians due to a fear of syncretism, which in turn leads them to accept the latter. That divine speech is directed to both animate and inanimate creation in Genesis 1 implies that such dualism does not belong to the narrative world. Welker concludes:

> The creature's own activity, which is itself a process of production, is not only a consequence and result of a creation that is already completed. Rather it is embedded in the process of creation and participates in that process.[81]

Such an insight reflects the H (and H-like) presumption that creation is unstable and that its unfolding is inherently risky. This is particularly evident in human (mis)agency in the Anthropocene.

In the Hebrew Bible, the rejection of the divinization/inanimate dualism extends to the land. Leviticus is potential source material for ethical reflection on the mutual responsibilities of

---

78. Fretheim, *God and World*, 37.
79. Welker, *Creation and Reality*, 13.
80. Joerstad, "Life of the World," 32.
81. Welker, *Creation and Reality*, 11.

Israel and the land in Sabbath keeping.[82] We have already seen that Sabbath is linked to creation (Exod 31:17; cf. Gen 2:1-3) and so cannot be for human rest alone.[83] In the creation account, as in Exodus 31, *hashamayim weet haarets* ("the heavens and the earth") is a merism for all that exists. The *erets* represents the dry land (*yabashah*, Gen 1:10) which brings forth plants (Gen 1:11-12) and the living creatures (Gen 1:24). In H, *erets* either refers to the land which the people enter and tend (e.g., Lev 25:2), or the land of Egypt from which they were rescued (e.g., Lev 18:3). The seventh year Sabbath is portrayed as being for the land (*laarets*) also to take a complete rest (*shabat shabaton*, Lev 25:4, 5). The land must observe a total cessation to *Yhwh* (*weshabetah haarets shabat layhwh*) from its customary vocation (Lev 25:2).[84] That the land is active in Sabbath keeping, rather than the passive recipient of human Sabbath observance, is suggested by comparison with Lev 23:32 where the people are to "celebrate your Sabbath" (*tishbetu shabattekem*).

The land has a relationship with *Yhwh* that precedes that between Israel and *Yhwh*, although now Israel and land share the same covenant with *Yhwh*.[85] Indeed, H stresses the divine ownership of the land over any Israelite claim (Lev 25:23).[86] There is a parallel between Leviticus 25 and the Priestly creation story: creation of the *erets* ("earth") by God precedes that of *haadam* (humans) just as *Yhwh* has prior relationship with the *erets* ("land") before the arrival of Israel. The *adam* as the divine image bearers are blessed to multiply, to subdue the *erets* (for agriculture) and have dominion (Gen 1:26-30). The *adam* is the divine image bearer in God's creation, with the implied responsibility to allow all the *erets* to enjoy the Sabbath (Gen 2:2-3). This Sabbath keeping was a reminder the divine ordering of chaos.

---

82. Cf. Morgan, "Transgressing, Puking, Covenanting," 173-74.
83. Fretheim, *God and World*, 60.
84. Stackert, "Sabbath of the Land," 243.
85. Morgan, "Transgressing, Puking, Covenanting," 178.
86. Stackert, "Sabbath of the Land," 247. The implications of the divine ownership of the land will be examined in more detail in the next chapter.

Hence, Israel's responsibility to keep the Sabbath is exercised in the context of divine ownership of both the people and the land. In vv. 4–5, there is a prohibition on the people of Israel sowing, pruning, or reaping because the seventh year is set aside as a complete rest for the land. While agricultural activity is forbidden, there was provision for gathering what the land yields during this time (vv. 6–7). However, Stackert points out that H promises sufficient provision during the sixth year, so that this need would not arise. This provision stands in stark contrast to the total rest for the land.[87] This rest is part of the divine order, and hence the responsibility of Israel to ensure it occurs, by its own Sabbath observance.

A further active role of the land is described in Lev 18:24–28, wherein land is portrayed as "a living being with its own personality," and "an entity distinct from its inhabitants."[88] Whether or not this personification is overstated, the land is active in judging Israel for its failure to keep the covenant. In vv. 24–25, the people are warned not to defile themselves (*al titammeru*) as did the nations (*nitmeu goyim*) in the land before them, as this in turn defiles the land (*watitma haarets*).

As a result of this transfer of defilement, the land is punished "for a failure to fulfil its obligation to God."[89] *Yhwh* "visits judgement" (*paqad*) not on the iniquity of the land's inhabitants, but on the iniquity of the land.[90] This judgement in turn flows from land to inhabitants. *Yhwh* is not described as judging inhabitants of the land. Instead, the land vomited out (*qo*) the nations (v. 25). This vomiting out (*qaah et haggo*) is a warning "lest the land vomit you out when you defile it" (*welo taqi haarets etkem betamaakem*, v. 28). There appears to be a two-way transfer occurring. Defilement is transferred from the inhabitants to the land, and the consequences of judgement are transferred from the land to the inhabitants. Such a vomiting out would be a break in the good

---

87. Stackert, "Sabbath of the Land," 243.
88. Joosten, *People and the Land in the Holiness Code*, 152.
89. Morgan, "Transgressing, Puking, Covenanting," 177.
90. The only other example of *paqad* being used with the land as direct or indirect object is Psalm 65:10. Joerstad, "Life of the World," 148.

order that Israel experienced while in the land, and is for them, a return to chaos.

The goal of this vomiting out is rest for the land. While Israel is in exile in the land of its enemies, the land shall enjoy its Sabbaths, making up for the times it did not rest on the Sabbaths of the Israelites (Lev 26:34–35). The verb *ratsah* ("enjoy") occurs 57 times in the Hebrew Bible, nine times in H, and five times in Leviticus 26. It is used often to describe divine pleasure or its lack in sacrifices.[91] It is also used of the favour of individuals or groups of people.[92] Its use for the land, therefore, is significant (see Lev 26:34, 43). The sense in v. 34 is that of enjoyment of Sabbath rest. In v. 41, it is used of the people accepting their guilt, in the sense of making amends, as it leads to *Yhwh* remembering the covenant (v. 42). Finally, *ratsah* is used twice in v. 43. Applied to the people, it is usually rendered "make amends," but when applied to the land it can be translated either as "enjoy" (as in v. 34, where a Qal imperfect is also used in the first example) or as "make amends." Given that the land has been punished for iniquity (Lev 18:25), either reading is possible. The land could be required to make up for its lost Sabbaths as a debt to *Yhwh*. The pairing with *ratsah* for the people is suggestive without being conclusive. The main point is that language used of *Yhwh* and humans, is once again applied to non-humans, i.e., it can either "enjoy" or "make amends" in a similar way to *Yhwh* and Israel. Therefore, the land is possibly being personified as having emotional experiences, if not ascribed agency and responsibility to make amends with *Yhwh* as part of a covenant relationship.

Either way, the exile restores the land to its covenant observance.[93] Of principal importance here is v. 42, where *Yhwh* promises to remember his covenant with Jacob, Isaac, and Abraham, but also to remember the land. Morgan understands this to mean that the land is not simply "a stage on which the drama of the covenant unfolds" but is itself a character that participates "in a web of

---

91. Lev 1:4; 7:18; 19:7; 22:23, 25, 27.
92. Deut 33:24; Esth 10:3; Job 20:10.
93. Joerstad, "Life of the World," 153.

mutually obligated covenant relationships with *YHWH* and with the people."[94] While there are obvious covenant obligations to keep the Sabbath, Lev 26:42 does not describe a *berith* ("covenant") between the land and *Yhwh*, in contrast with the threefold usage applied to the Patriarchs. However, the status of the land as "mine," in contrast to Israel as aliens and tenants, identifies a pre-existing relationship (Lev 25:23). The mutual covenant of Israel and the land with *Yhwh* is implicit in their shared need to keep the Sabbath. Israel's observance of the Sabbath "leaves space for the land to practise its obedience to *YHWH*."[95] Hence, Israel's agricultural activities and Sabbath practices are constrained by the need for the land to observe its own Sabbath.

Conclusion

In this chapter, I have shown that the creation story in Genesis is most likely a Holiness School (H) reworking of a Priestly *chaoskampf*. The emphasis of H is on the Sabbath, which is effected by the imposition of six days of creation on eight creative acts, and the addition of Gen 1:3–5 and 2:2–3. Sabbath keeping is implied by the sanctifying of the seventh day and the creation of sacred time, but is not fully articulated. This command as imitative of the divine Sabbath is taken up in H (Lev 17–26). The underlying *chaoskampf* points in two directions. Firstly, after other Near Eastern creation myths, God is installed in a temple. This, similar to Sabbath keeping, is more protological than actual. The connection to the Tabernacle is via the so-called completion formulae. Secondly, Sabbath keeping is a mimetic way of maintaining order over and against the forces of chaos. Sabbath serves as a reminder to the people of their covenant status before *Yhwh*, but also reminds *Yhwh* of covenant obligations, foremost of which in Leviticus 23 is the provision of seasonal rains and good harvest. Further, both Sabbath and temple come together in H. Sabbath is both for the

---

94. Morgan, "Transgressing, Puking, Covenanting," 178.
95. Morgan, "Transgressing, Puking, Covenanting," 178.

observance of the laity, but also the provision of temple service; i.e., holiness is about keeping the Sabbath and revering the Sanctuary (Lev 19:30).

Beyond Israel's obligation to keep the Sabbath, the land is also required to observe its own Sabbath. The *erets* as earth in Genesis 1 plays a role in its own unfolding, namely bringing forth vegetation and living creatures. In H, *erets* as land must observe its Sabbath rest, and vomit out its inhabitants when they fail to be holy. If, as I will claim in chapter 3, human care for creation is an expression of holiness, then failure to care properly can similarly result in the *erets* as earth vomiting humanity out.

Land brings forth its abundance when it is given rest, when not polluted by its inhabitants, and when it is watered by *Yhwh*. The land is *Yhwh*'s, and not Israel's. The combination of Genesis 1 and the Holiness Code suggests, in effect, that the land cannot finally be dominated. Against appearances, it is quietly stronger than the humans. Implications for doing theology in the Anthropocene will be developed in chapter 4, but first we need to meditate on the contribution of the second creation narrative in Genesis.

3

The Holy Garden

Introduction

ANY THEOLOGICAL TREATMENT OF the problem Anthropocene would be incomplete without a discussion of the Garden story of Genesis 2–3. In particular, Norman Habel identifies texts like Gen 2:15 as supportive of an earth-centered ethic, a so-called "green text," in comparison to the "grey text" of Gen 1:26–28, which has been used to justify practices characteristic of the Anthropocene.[1] Having shown that the Priestly creation story is more green than grey, we now turn to Genesis 2–3.

This chapter examines the non-Priestly Garden story,[2] which Nicholas Wyatt notes is "one of the foundation documents of western culture," and has been influential in Christian, Jewish, and Muslim thought.[3] However, Western readers have often interpreted

1. Habel, *Inconvenient Text*, xvii.

2. The Documentary Hypothesis has traditionally identified at least four sources in the Pentateuch, two of which are found in the Primeval History. I have already discussed the P and H sources in the previous chapter. The Yahwist (J) hypothesis accounts for much of Genesis 2–11, but this model has proven highly problematic. As early as Wellhausen, J was understood as having gone through various editions. This variety had led some scholars have abandoned the idea of J altogether, as Thomas Römer does. It will be sufficient for this chapter to identify a non-P source that uses Yhwh Elohim to identify God. See Römer, "Elusive Yahwist," 9–27.

3. Wyatt, "Royal Garden," 1–35.

the text in ways that are foreign to its original context.[4] There are many elements of the text that suggest the original authors understood the narrative very differently—as relating to their own time, and not to a paradisiac prelapsarian past.[5] In this chapter, I pose four exegetical questions with which to interrogate the text from an earth perspective, before introducing modern hermeneutical concerns in chapter 4.

First, what does the Garden story tell us about the relationship of the *adam* to the soil? I will argue that Gen 2:4 is an editorial join between P's creation account (as discussed in chapter 2) and the Garden story that introduces the earth family, of which the *adam* is a part. Further, the *adam* is created for the sake of the earth.

Secondly, what role does Eden play in this relationship? Here, I identify Eden with the temple sanctuary. The *adam*'s creation from the dust of the earth represents a coronation to a sacral kingship. Care of the garden represents cultic responsibility, while also being attentive to the needs of the soil outside of the temple precincts.

Thirdly, how does this relationship change outside of the Garden in the rest of the Primeval History? Ejection from the Garden represents exile, but the continuing tending of the soil demonstrates an ongoing relationship with *Yhwh* outside of the land. The Garden story itself hints at such a broader concern for life outside.

Finally, how is this relationship reenvisaged in the Holiness Code (H) in Leviticus 26? Here we see the possibility of the Edenization of Canaan, i.e., the extension of the holiness of the sanctuary to include the entire land. This has the implication of considering earth care as part of Israelite holiness. The command to keep the Sabbath and reverence the sanctuary includes providing Sabbath rest for the land as an expression of lay holiness. Hence, I argue that Leviticus 26 brings together the P and non-P stories of Genesis 1–3 in a concern for the earth.

---

4. See Zevit, *What Really Happened in the Garden of Eden?*, xxvii.
5. Wyatt, "Royal Garden," 1.

From Creation to Canaan

The Adam and the Soil

The Earth Family: The *toledot* Formula in Genesis 2:4

The Garden story begins in Gen 2:5, extending through Gen 3:24.[6] Genesis 2:4 is best understood as an editorial addition, framing the story that follows as the creation of the adam (*haadam*) as part of the earth (*haarets*) family. This filial relationship carries with it responsibilities. Two arguments supporting v. 4 as an introduction are worth stating briefly.[7] Firstly, v. 5a compares more closely than v. 4b with similar clauses in *Enuma Elish* and Sumerian creation stories. While v. 4b contains a similar dependent clause *beyom* ("in the day"),[8] these stories also contain an initial negative evaluation of the world prior to the creation of humans. This matches v. 5a

---

6. Tryggve Mettinger notes that the key motifs that tie the text from Genesis 2:5 to 3:34 include dust (2:7 with 3:23) and the tree of life and the tree of life (2:9; 2:22, 24). Mettinger, *Eden Narrative*, 13–14.

7. Stephen Kempf notes features of v. 4 that appear to suggest for a split. Genesis 2:4a shares the vocabulary of what proceeds it, forming a chiasm with the reversal of *hashamayim wehaarets* and *bara* in 1:1: *bara Elohim et hashamayim wehaarets* 1:1 / *hashamayim wehaarets behibaeram* 2:4a. This connection has led to suggestions that v. 4a was the original heading to the Gen 1:1—2:3, which is speculative, or the ending; Kempf, "Introducing the Garden of Eden," 39–40. Against the later argument, we saw in the last chapter that the Sabbath etiology of Gen 2:2–3 is reinforced by the heptadic use of various words. Inclusion of v. 4 would break the heptadic structure of *erets*. Kempf himself identifies a chiasmus between v. 4a and 4b that suggests that verse is a unity: *shamayim wehaarets behibaeram* // *asot Yhwh Elohim hashamayim wearets*. While there is a change in v. 4b from *bara* to *asah*, this does not indicate a change in author. The verb *asah* is found both in P's creation account where it is used interchangeably with *bara*, and the non-P Garden story. In P, see Gen 1:7, 11–12, 16, 25–26, 31; 2:2–3. In non-P, see Gen 2:18; 3:1, 7, 13–14, 21. Finally, Terje Stordalen notes that the shift in order from "the heavens and the earth" to "the earth and the heavens," is not an argument for separate authors on source critical grounds. P is understood to post-date the non-P Garden story, and so the shift cannot be the result of the non-P author changing P's order, as they would have been unaware of it. See Stordalen, "Genesis 2,4," 165–66.

8. Kempf, "Introducing the Garden of Eden," 40.

better than does 4b.⁹ As Terje Stordalen notes, the "when not yet" formula is typical for "stories of primaeval times."¹⁰

Secondly, Stephen Kempf points out that v. 4 contains a chiasmus, which demonstrates both its unity and purpose. The key clauses are:

> v. 4a: *hashamayim wehaarats behibaream* ("The heavens and the earth when they were created")

> v. 4b: *asowt Yhwh Elohim erets weshamayim* ("*Yhwh* God made earth and the heavens").

The swapping of *erets* ("earth") before *shamayim* ("heavens") indicates a shift of frame of reference from the entire cosmos to focus on the earth.¹¹ This shift in frame of reference is marked using the noun *toledot*. The word *toledot* is typically translated as "generations" and is referred to as the *toledot* formula as it is the book of Genesis' "most salient literary marker," acting as "a connective heading that opens a new unit concerning a familiar figure and the descendants of that figure."¹² This formula occurs eleven times in the book of Genesis. Four occurrences in the Primeval History parallel its usage in Gen 2:4.¹³ Genesis 2:4 and 5:1 follow a similar pattern:¹⁴

> Gen 2:4: These are the generations [*eleh toledot*] of the heavens and the earth, in the day [*beyom*] that *Yhwh* God made [*asowt*] the earth and heavens.

---

9. Stordalen, "Genesis 2,4," 168.

10. Stordalen, "Man, Soil, Garden," 9.

11. Kempf, "Introducing the Garden of Eden," 40. Stordalen also argues that the reversed *erets weshamiyim* as the narrative form, compared to the preceding idiomatic form appropriate for creation stories. See Stordalen, "Genesis 2,4," 175.

12. Schwartz, "Narrative *Toledot* Formulae in Genesis."

13. Gen 5:1; 6:9; 10:1; 11:10, 27; 25:12, 19; 36:1, 9; Num 3:1; Ruth 4:18; 1 Chr 1:29. Stordalen, "Genesis 2,4," 169.

14. This is an interpretation Kempf struggles with, despite noting the structural similarities in the use of *toledot* throughout. Kempf, "Introducing the Garden of Eden," 39.

Gen 5:1: This is the book of the generations [*zeh sepher toledot*] of Adam, in the day [*beyom*] God made [*bero*] Adam in the likeness of God he made him.

Both verses contain two halves, the first of which includes whose *toledot* is being described. The second half of both verses begins with the temporal clause *beyom* together with *bara* or *asah*. Stordalen comments that Gen 5:1 introduces a new genealogy that partly overlaps that of Gen 4:17–26, dealing in more detail with the line of Seth.[15] This pattern of introducing material which is similar but different to that which preceded it is consistent with the other occurrences of *toledot* in the Primeval History.[16] The *toledot* of Gen 2:4 observes this same pattern. There is a chiasmus between v. 4a and Gen 1:1 with a shift in the position of *bara* ("create"):

Gen 1:1: *bara Elohim et hashamayim weet haarets* ("God created the heavens and the earth")

Gen 2:4a: *hashamayim wehaarets behibaream* ("The heavens and the earth when they were created")

This indicates that what follows deals with the preceding account by covering similar but different details, a different perspective on the *toledot* of the *erets*.

In light of these conclusions, it is important to ask whether we can adopt a procreative interpretation for *toledot* in Gen 2:4; i.e., can the earth be a progenitor for what follows, including humans?[17] As noted in the last chapter, there is a tendency to ignore or downplay the agency of non-human creation. The Garden

---

15. Stordalen, "Genesis 2,4," 173.

16. Genesis 10:1 introduces the *toledot* of Noah's sons, compare 9:18–27, and in 11:10 another *toledot* of Shem. Stordalen notes that of the instances of *toledot* in the Primeval History, Gen 6:9 appears not to fit the pattern. This verse appears to introduce the story of Noah himself and not his sons. Stordalen suggests that to maintain coherence, the genealogy is limited to 6:10. Likewise, 6:9b provides extra information about Noah in the way in which the temporal clauses do in 2:4 and 5:1, compare *bedorotah* ("in his generations") with *beyom* ("in the day"). However, the preceding passage mentions nothing of Noah's line, only himself (Gen 6:8). Stordalen, "Genesis 2,4," 170–71.

17. Contra Stordalen, "Genesis 2,4," 176–77.

story portrays *Yhwh Elohim* in anthropomorphic terms, forming, planting, and making. The role of the *adamah* as the material source for the *adam*, plants, and non-human animals is prefigured in the placing of *erets* first in Gen 2:4b.

From and for the Soil

The Garden story begins in Gen 2:5, introducing a problem for the soil (*adamah*), for which the creation of the Adam (*haadam*) is part of the solution. The negative formula *terem yiyeh* ("before there was") accompanied by an explanatory phrase beginning with *ki* ("for") is used on four other occasions besides v. 5 to indicate events yet to have occurred.[18] The structure of v. 5 is thus:

> a: *wekol siach hasadeh terem yiyah baarets* ("when not plant of the field was yet in the earth").
>
> b: *wekal eseb hasedah terem yitsmah* ("and no herb of the field had yet sprung up").
>
> c: *ki lo himtir Yhwh Elohim al haarets* ("for *Yhwh* God had not caused it to rain on the ground").
>
> d: *weadam ayin laabod et haadamah* ("and there was no Adam to till the ground").

The noun *erets* is most often used in the Primeval History to refer to the whole Earth.[19] The *sadeh* ("field") can refer specifically to cultivated fields (Gen 4:10; 9:3; Hos 12:12) or non-agricultural land where wild animals dwell (Gen 25:27, 29; Lev 26:22). In Gen 2:5, the *sadeh* is where vegetation grows, both *siach* and *eseb*. *Siach* occurs only three times outside of v. 5, where it likely refers to wild, uncultivated vegetation.[20] The lack of *siach* (v. 5a) is due to the lack of rain on the *erets* (v. 5b).

---

18. Exod 9:30; 10:7; Isa 7:16; 8:4. Stordalen, "Man, Soil, Garden," 9.

19. Stordalen, "Man, Soil, Garden," 11. It can also refer to specific land (Gen 2:11–12) or be identified with dry land (*yabashah*) to distinguish it from the sea (Gen 1:10).

20. In Gen 21:15, Hagar places Ishmael under a *siach* in the *midbar*

By contrast, *eseb* likely refers to cultivated plants.[21] The lack of *eseb* (v. 5b) is due to the lack of the *adam* to *abad* ("cultivate") the *adamah* ("soil"). This relationship between *adam*, *eseb*, and *abad* is also described in Ps 104:14–15:

> You cause the grass to grow for the cattle, and plants [*eseb*] for people to use [lit. "for the service (*abad*) of the *adam*"], to bring forth food from the earth, and wine to gladden the human heart.

Here, plants (*eseb*) are serving (*abad*) human needs and grass for cattle are both caused to grow (*matsmiyah*, Hiphil of *tsamach*) by God. The end products of the *erets* are *lechem* (translated as both food and bread), wine, and oil. Similar language is found in the cursing of the *erets* (Gen 3:18–19):

> Thorns and thistles it shall bring forth [*tatsmiyah*] for you; and you shall eat the plants of the field [*eseb hasadeh*]. By the sweat of your face you shall eat bread [*lechem*] until you return to the ground [*haadamah*], for out of it you were taken; you are dust [*aphar*], and to dust you shall return.

Here, *lechem* is the result of toil. Rather than the *erets* as the source of nourishment and *eseb*, it provides thorns and thistles and acts as a reminder of mortality, when humans revert to *aphar* ("dust").

We can now begin to see how the *toledot* formula introduces a genealogy of the *erets* (Gen 2:4b). One line follows from *erets* ("earth") to the *adam* by causing rain on the *siach* ("field"). Without rain (*matar*) the field is absent of arable soil, and hence vegetation. This is Stordalen's logic of the spatial matrix of *erets* → *siach* → *adamah*.[22] Graphically, this may be illustrated in the figure below.

("wilderness") of Beersheba. A *midbar* can variously represent uninhabited land (Job 38:26), or land used for pasture (Joel 2:22). Job 30 describes a famine, where people flee to the wilderness to eat tree roots and mallow by the bushes (*siach*, v. 4).

21. There are thirty-three occurrences of this verb in the Hebrew Bible, and only Jer 14:6 and 2 Kgs 19:26 clearly refer to wild plants. Stordalen, "Man, Soil, Garden," 10.

22. Stordalen, "Man, Soil, Garden," 12.

FIGURE 1

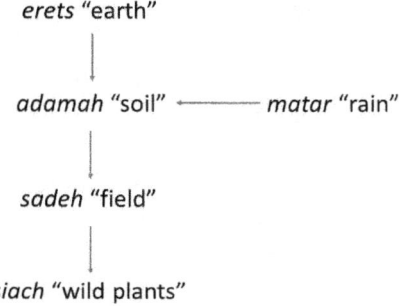

The generations of the *erets* leading to wild plants.

The second line leads to the *adamah* and cultivated plants (*eseb*). This is more complicated than the generation of non-agricultural vegetation due to the reciprocal relationship between the *adam* and the *adamah*:

FIGURE 2

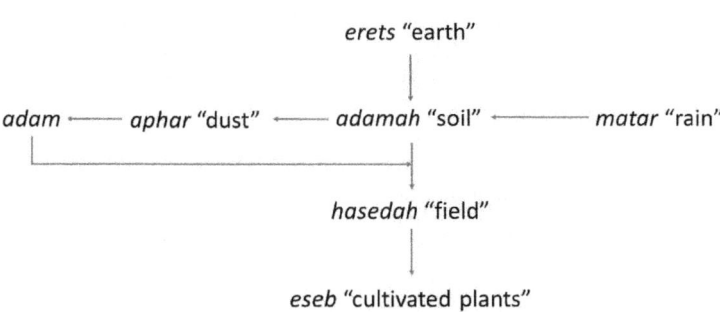

The generations of the *erets* leading to cultivated plants.

Here, the *adam* is formed from the *adamah* which first required rain (*matar*) so that the dust (*aphar*) could be moulded by *Yhwh* as a potter would clay. In turn, the *adam* acts to cultivate the ground (*laabod et haadamah*) to produce herbs of the field (*eseb hasadeh*).

Central to my argument is that the noun *ed* (Gen 2:6) can be translated as cloud, providing rain (*matar*) both for the *siach* and the *aphar*. The only other occurrence of *ed* is in Job 36:27, and attempts to clarify the meaning are inconclusive. Stordalen claims that *ed* is an underground river, which feeds the river that waters the Garden, and—only incidentally—the lands outside.[23] This watering does not correspond to the lack of rain in v. 5, and hence it is entirely directed towards wetting the dust from which the *adam* is formed.[24]

However, a better solution is that provided by Max Rogland, who demonstrates than in Rabbinic literature, *ed* is part of "the semantic field of clouds."[25] He further observes that Ps 135:7 and Jer 10:13 provide an intertextual argument for *ed* as cloud, even though the word itself does not appear in these verses. The three passages are:

> Ps 135:7: "he who makes the clouds rise at the end of the earth [*maaleh nesiim mistseh haarets*] who makes lightnings for the rain [*matar*] and brings out the wind from his storehouses."

> Jer 10:13: "and he makes the mist rise from the ends of the earth [*weyaaleh nesiim miqtseh erets haarets*]. He makes lightnings for the rain [*matar*] and brings out the wind from his storehouses."

> Gen 2:6 :"but a stream would rise from the earth and water [*waed yaaleh min haarets wehishqah*] the whole face of the ground."

---

23. Stordalen, "Man, Soil, Garden," 13, 17.

24. Stordalen, "Man, Soil, Garden," 14. Note that the lack of rain or wetted soil for the divine potter makes Kidner's argument for an initially wet earth to match the story of Genesis 1 implausible. See Kidner, "Genesis 2:5,6," 109–14.

25. Rogland, "Interpreting אד in Genesis 2.5–6," 385.

In Ps 135:7 and Jer 10:13, *hiphil* forms (indicating causative action) of *alah* ("ascend") are used to describe the vapors being raised by God from the ends of the *erets*, resulting in rain, lightning, and wind. Note the inconsistency of the NRSV in translating *nesiim* as clouds (Ps 135:7) or mist (Jer 10:13). In Gen 2:6, the *ed* rises *min haarets* ("from the earth") to water (*shaqah*) the face of the earth. Theses similarities suggest that *ed* is equivalent to *nesiim* and the watering to rainfall. In both the Psalm and Jeremiah passage, creation language is employed, strengthening the intertextual links.[26] In Jer 10:12, the familiar merism earth and heaven is used: *oseh erets* ("he has made earth") ... *natah shamayim* ("he has stretched out the heavens"). Likewise, referring to divine sovereignty, the Psalmist invokes Genesis 1: *bashamayim ubaarets bayamim wekal tehomot* ("in heaven and on earth, in the seas and all deeps," v. 6). Hence, while there is a strong focus on the role of the *adam* in cultivating the *adamah* and the Garden, the broader *erets* is not neglected as Stordalen suggests.

This point is significant because it makes better sense of what follows in vv. 7-9. Just as the *toledot* of *adam* splits at Noah into multiple lines, so the *toledot* of *erets* now splits. The rain from the *ed* allows wild vegetation to grow and the creation of *haadam*. In v. 7, *Yhwh* God forms the *adam* (Qal of *yatsar*) from the dust of the ground (*aphar min haadamah*) and breaths into him the breath of life. In v. 9, *Yhwh* God then plants a garden and makes grow (Hiphil of *tsamach*) every tree out of the ground (*min haadamah kal ets*). The growing of trees (*ets*) from the *adamah* and the forming of the *adam* were both made possible by rain. Both humans and trees are therefore separate lines of the *toledot*, as are the beasts and birds that are also formed *min hadamah* (v. 19).

---

26. Rogland, "Interpreting אד in Genesis 2.5-6," 388.

FIGURE 3

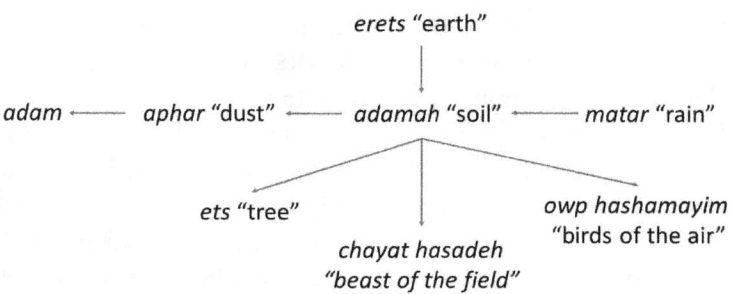

The generations of the *erets* leading to various living beings.

The *adam* in the Garden

The Garden story draws a strong connection between the creation of the *adam* and the tending of the *adamah*. The lack of a servant (*abad*) of the *erets* in Gen 2:5 is apparently fulfilled in Gen 3:23. Now I will argue that the placing of the *adam* in the Garden is central to this plot, not a distraction from it.[27] Peter Feinman notes that the "location of Eden has spawned a cottage industry of its own."[28] He lists five different approaches, several of which are non-exclusive.[29] Here I argue that the Garden of Eden is not a mythic, primordial location, but is rather an archetypal sanctuary.[30] As such it is a place where *Yhwh* dwells and is to be worshipped by the *adam* who serves in the royal garden in Jerusalem as a sacral king.[31] Such kingly responsibilities include oversight of the *erets* outside of the Garden.

---

27. Contra Stordalen, "Man, Soil, Garden," 15.
28. Feinman, "Analysis," 178.
29. Feinman, "Analysis," 172–73.
30. See, e.g., Wenham, "Sanctuary Symbolism," 399–404.
31. See Brueggemann, "From Dust to Kingship," 1–18; LeFebrve, "Adam Reigns in Eden," 25–57; Wyatt, "Royal Garden," 21.

The Garden as the Jerusalem Sanctuary

A clue to the Garden's location in Jerusalem is the name Eden, which is associated with Hebrew words that mean "luxury."[32] An old Aramaic verb form *'dn* seems to mean "who enriches, gives abundance," and it is used in connection with the god Hadad, who is described as "water-controller of heaven and earth, who rains down plenty" and as "water-controller of all rivers."[33] This is consistent with the emphasis in Genesis 2 on water—both the *ed* "raincloud" and the river that waters Eden (Gen 2:10). The well-watered nature of Eden is recalled in Lot's appraisal of the Jordan Valley (Gen 13:10) as *kegan Yhwh* ("like the Garden of *Yhwh*").

The identification of the four rivers also provides a strong clue to the location of Eden. Debate centers around the location of the Gihon (Gen 2:13). Its significance may have shifted over time, as the Garden story has likely been subject to significant editorial activity.[34] Feinman identifies the Gihon with the Nile, arguing that it is "inconceivable that a biblical author either in the land of Canaan or in Mesopotamia excluded the Nile River from this four-river world view." Jerusalem is not the cosmic center at creation but becomes so in historic time.[35] He understands that the addition of "in the East" (Gen 2:8) reorients the reader from Egypt to Dilmun.[36] However, Wyatt identifies the Gihon with the Gihon in Jerusalem. He notes that the identification of Gihon with the Nile with certainty dates to the Greek translation in 300 BCE.[37] There are references to a local Gihon supplying Jerusalem with water and

---

32. An older view is that it is based on a Sumerian word, via Akkadian, meaning "plain" or "steppe." However, A. R. Millard identifies some problems with this. The first is a lack of ayin in Sumerian and no evidence that one stood at the beginning of the Akkadian word. Secondly, the word is rare in Akkadian and other words are used to render the Sumerian. Millard, "Etymology of Eden," 104–5.

33. Millard, "Etymology of Eden," 105.
34. See Thompson, "Yahwist Creation Story," 188.
35. Feinman, "Analysis," 184–85.
36. Feinman, "Analysis," 181.
37. Wyatt, "Royal Garden," 11.

being used in royal rituals (1 Kgs 1:33, 38; Ps 110:7). There is also a possible allusion in Psalm 36, where associated with *Yhwh*'s house (or temple, *bayith*) is "a river of your delights" (*nachal adaneka*).³⁸ The noun delights is based on the root Eden. This places Jerusalem firmly in the cosmic center, which is consistent with it being the sanctuary of *Yhwh*.

Several texts associated Eden with the temple sanctuary. Firstly, in Ezekiel 28, the King of Tyre is described as having been *beeden gan Elohim* ("in Eden the garden of God," Ezek 28:13). Lexical links between Ezekiel 28 and the Garden include reference to the precious stones and gold of Havilah (v. 13; cf. Gen 2:11–12) and the cherubim (v. 14; cf. Gen 3:24).³⁹ The geographical reference "holy mountain of God" hints at the temple mount, although a sacred mountain with vegetation and water is a "stock motif in ancient Near Eastern iconography."⁴⁰

A second geographical reference is that the Garden was entered from the east (Gen 3:24). It is likely this was the only entrance, otherwise the placing of the cherubim there to guard it (*shamar*) would be redundant. Wyatt assumes that the cherubim were already there but were only noticed when the human pair were ejected.⁴¹ This is unclear, particularly given the *adam* was placed in the garden (Gen 2:15) also to guard it (*shamar*). The entrance to the tent of meeting was to the east (Num 3:28), as was the entrance to the temple in Jerusalem (Ezek 8:16). It is also significant that in Ezekiel's vision of the glory leaving the temple, the cherubim depart from the East Gate.

Thirdly, Gordon Wenham observes that these guardian cherubim (Gen 3:24) feature in Solomon's temple in the inner sanctuary

---

38. Wyatt, "Royal Garden," 12.

39. It is curious that while Mettinger can identify "both the first man and the king of Tyre were figures of peculiar arrogance," he does not identify both as royal. Mettinger, *Eden Narrative*, 96.

40. Mettinger, *Eden Narrative*, 15.

41. Wyatt, "Royal Garden," 18.

The Holy Garden

(1 Kgs 6:23–28), decorate the walls (1 Kgs 6:29) and doors (1 Kgs 6:32), and top the Ark of the Covenant (Exod 25:18–22).[42]

Fourthly, the divine presence in both Eden and sanctuary is indicated by *Yhwh* walking to and fro within them. The *hithpael* (reflexive) of *halak* (Gen 3:8), is also used in connection with the Tabernacle being carried with the people (2 Sam 7:6–7) and the presence among the people (Lev 26:12; Deut 23:14).[43]

A final thematic link is trees. Michaela Bauks notes that trees are a common indicator of holy places where the human and divine meet.[44] Wenham identifies several tree related themes between the Garden and the temple.[45] The tree of life represents fullness of life. The association of fullness of life with the sanctuary underlies the sacrificial law and is a theme in the Psalms. The life of a creature is in its blood, and this blood was not to be consumed but was used to make atonement, and hence save life (Lev 17:10–14). Psalm 24 contains creation language (vv. 1–2), and refers to the temple mount as "the hill of *Yhwh*" (*har Yhwh*) as a holy place (*maqom qadesho*, v. 3) where blessing is received (v. 5).

Wenham also suggests the lampstand is a stylized tree of life (Exod 25:31–35). Given Exodus 25 also mentions the cherubim (vv. 18–22), this association is quite possible. The tree of knowledge of good and evil is pleasing to the sight (*nechmad lemareh*, Gen 2:9), pleasant to the eyes (*taawah hu leenayim*, Gen 3:6) and desirable to make one wise (*wenechmad lehaskil*, Gen 3:6). All these concepts are applied to the law (*torah*). In Ps 19:7–8, the law of *Yhwh* (*torah Yhwh*) enlighten the eyes (*meirat enayim*) and makes wise (*machimat*) the simple. The tablets of the law were kept in the ark (Exod 25:16) with the Book of the Law (*sepher torah*) beside it (Deut 31:26) in the holy of holies (Exod 26:34).

---

42. Wenham, "Sanctuary Symbolism," 401. LeFebrve, "Adam Reigns in Eden," 32.
43. Wenham, "Sanctuary Symbolism," 401.
44. Bauks, "Sacred Trees in the Garden of Eden," 280.
45. Wenham, "Sanctuary Symbolism," 401.

From Creation to Canaan

The *adam* as King

Now that we have placed Eden in Jerusalem, and associated it with the temple sanctuary, what does this imply for the role of the *adam* in the Garden? We have already seen that kingship is connected to the Garden (Ezek 28), and the river (1 Kgs 1:33, 38; Ps 110:7). Further, of the twenty-nine occurrences of the noun *gan* ("garden") outside of Genesis 2–3, eight refer to the king's garden.[46] This association suggests that the *adam* possesses royal status.

Walter Brueggemann associates the creation of the *adam* in Gen 2:7 with the bestowal of kingship.[47] While trees, beasts, and birds (Gen 2:9, 19) are formed *min haadamah* ("from the earth"), the *adam* is formed *aphar min haadamah* ("from the dust of the earth"). Brueggemann argues that *aphar* ("dust") describes pre-royal status based on three parallel passages:[48]

> Gen 2:7: *Yhwh* God formed the *adam* out of the dust of the ground [*min aphar haarets*].
>
> Gen 2:15: To tend and guard [*leabedah umeshamerah*] the garden of Eden.[49]
>
> 1 Kgs 16:2: I lifted you out of the dust [*min haaphar*] and made you ruler [*nagid*] over my people.
>
> 1 Sam 2:8 // Ps 113:7–8: He raises up the poor from the dust [*meaphar*]; and he lifts the needy from the ash heap to set them among princes [*nebidim*].

Individuals begin as *aphar* and are elevated to royal status, either ruler (*nagid*; 1 Kgs 16:2) or among princes (*nebedim*; 1 Sam 2:8; Ps 113:8), i.e., equal in rank. These parallels suggest that Gen 2:7 describes the bestowal of kingship on the *adam*. However, it is not clear that kingship exhausts the significance of *aphar*, either pre or post kingship. Brueggemann argues further that if *aphar* refers to

---

46. 2 Kgs 9:27; 21:18 (2x), 26; 25:4; Neh 3:15; Jer 39:4; 52:7.
47. Brueggemann, "From Dust to Kingship," 2.
48. Brueggemann, "From Dust to Kingship," 4.
49. Translation here is my own.

a pre-royal status, so it also applies to that of a deposed king. This view is more problematic.

In Gen 3:14, *aphar* is literal dust, the diet of the serpent. In v. 19, the *adam* eats bread by the sweat of his brow until "you return to the ground [*adamah*] for out of it you were taken [*luqacheta*]." Here, *laqach* recalls Gen 2:15 where the *adam* is taken from outside and placed in the Garden. As such, in v. 19 *laqach* could represent exile; i.e., removal from the Garden back to the outside, but it refers ultimately to death. Further, *aphar* is both the *adam's* present status of "dust you are" (*aphar atah*) and destination "and to dust you shall return" (*weel aphar tashub*). The first statement could be understood to say that the *adam* has now lost his kingly status, and what follows is the result or expression of this, exile from the Garden. A more likely reading is that *aphar* reflects human mortality, and that ejection from the Garden is *both* a loss of kingly status *and* leads to an inevitable death.⁵⁰

---

50. Brueggemann's parallel passages add little to this argument. In 1 Kgs 15:33–34, judgement is announced against Baasha, king of Israel. In 1 Kgs 16:1–7, *aphar* describes Baasha's pre-kingly but not post-kingly status. If it is implied, it is ambiguous. Baasha dies on the throne and sleeps with his ancestors. Is his death his dethronement or is judgment delated until his line ends in exile? 1 Sam 2:6–8a hints that *aphar* refers to non-kingly status, but possibly also refers to death. The passage presents a series of parallels:

v. 6: Yhwh kills and brings to life [*mechayah*], he brings down [*morid*] to Sheol and raises up [*weyaal*]

v. 7: Yhwh makes poor and makes rich; he brings low [*mashpil*], he also exalts [*meromem*].

v. 8a: He raises up [*meqim*] the poor from the dust [*meaphar*]; and he lifts [*meqim*] the needy from the ash heap to set them among princes.

Verse 7 clearly parallels "poor" with "low," and "making rich' with "exaltation," and the raising of the "poor" from the dust/ash heap life "among princes" in v. 8. It is also clear that v. 6 parallels kills/brings down to Sheol with brings to life/raises up (from Sheol). Yet two things mitigate against arguing that v. 6 is parallel with vv. 7–8a. Firstly, the proper noun Yhwh begins verses 6 and 7, suggesting they are to be treated as separate clauses, whereas the verb *meqim* in v. 8 has no subject, suggesting continuity with v. 7. Secondly, the Hebrew *mechayeh* ("makes alive") is the Piel participle masculine singular of *chayah* ("live"). The only other use of the Piel participle masculine singular is found in Neh 9:6 where it clearly refers to creation. It is therefore not clear that *mechayeh* means undoing death in a metaphorical sense parallel to being

In summary, Brueggemann is right to note a connection between creation of the *adam* from *aphar* and kingship, but by his own admission this connection does not exhaust the significance of *aphar*. It also refers to the essential nature of human being, an "affirmation that man is a one with the soil," as Brueggemann states.[51] In particular, that the *adam* is *aphar min haadamah* (Gen 2:7) both expresses a kinship with other creatures made *min haadamah* and points to the importance of the *adamah* for the human vocation.

The King as Gardener

If the *adam* is a king, how is tending and guarding the garden an exercise of royal rule? Throughout the Ancient Near East, palaces were built among gardens. The Book of Esther describes the Persian king exiting from a feast into the palace garden (Esth 7:7). Nebuchadnezzar built his hanging gardens of Babylon as a display of royal management.[52] Therefore, just as a king's palace and gardens were a symbol of rule and management beyond the palace itself to the entire kingdom, so the *adam* as gardener points to a broader rule and hence responsibility for the *adamah* beyond the garden. However, the king as gardener also alludes to cultic duties.[53]

One of the lexical keys to understanding the cultic role of the *adam* is *leabedah uleshamerah* (Gen 2:15). The verb *abad* is sometimes used in the agricultural sense; i.e., to "till" or "tend." As the pair are ejected from the Garden, the *adam* is told that he is "to till the ground from which he had been taken" (*leabod et haadamah asher luqah*, Gen 3:23). Cain is described as a tiller of

---

elevated to royalty. Further, of the sixty-six occurrences of *Sheol* ("grave") in the Hebrew Bible, none appear to be figurative. Indeed, while 1 Sam 2:6 speaks of God "raising" (*weyaal*, from *Sheol*), Job 7:9 claims the dead are not raised (*lo yaaleh*). It is therefore clear that dust means poor/lowly as opposed to exalted, but that this not clearly equated with death.

51. Brueggemann, "From Dust to Kingship," 2.
52. LeFebvre, "Adam Reigns in Eden," 30–31.
53. Wyatt, "Royal Garden," 24.

the ground (*abad adamah*, Gen 4:2).⁵⁴ *Abad* is most often used in the context of service, to a king (2 Sam 16:19) or to *Yhwh*. In Exod 3:12, *Yhwh*'s proof to Israel that he is sending Moses to them is that "you shall serve (*taabdun*) God on this mountain."⁵⁵ Particularly relevant to this discussion, *abad* is also used in connection with the Tabernacle (Num 4:37, 41).

The verb *shamar* is used to refer to animal husbandry (1 Sam 17:20), guarding a place or person (1 Kgs 14:27; 20:39), divine protection (Ps 121:7–8), and the preservation of food (Gen 41:35). It also describes obedience to all *Yhwh*'s statutes (*weshamarta kal chukaw*, Exod 15:26) and covenant (*ushemartem et berithi*, Exod 19:5). Specifically, when the verbs *abad* and *shamar* are used together outside of Gen 2:15, they refer to Levitical sanctuary service.⁵⁶ Numbers 3:7–8 describes Levitical functions as it relates to Aaron, the people, and the Tabernacle and its furnishings.

> They shall perform duties for him [*weshameru et mishmartow*] and for the whole congregation in front of the tent of meeting, doing service [*laabod et abodat*] at the Tabernacle; they shall be in charge of [*weshameru*] all the furnishings of the tent of meeting, and attend to the duties [*weshameru*] for the Israelites as they do service [*abodat*] at the Tabernacle.

The Levites are to attend (*weshameru*, from *shamar*) to the needs (*mishmartow*) of Aaron and the whole congregation before the tent of meeting, and to do the work (*laabod et abodat*, from *abad*) of the Tabernacle (v. 7). The same verb, *weshameru*, is used to describe how the Levites are to approach all of the Tabernacle furnishings and the needs of the sons of Israel.

This verb is rendered in the NRSV as "in charge of" when referring to the furnishings, but "attend to" or "perform duties for" when referring to humans, all of whom have needs (*mishmartow*). However, *mishmartow* has as its object both the furnishings and

54. See also for example, Deut 28:39; Prov 12:11; 28:19.
55. See also Exod 3:12; 4:23; 7:16; 8:1, 20; 9:1, 13; 10:3, 7, 8, 11, 24, 26; 12:31.
56. Wenham, "Sanctuary Symbolism," 401.

the needs of those who are performing temple service. Likewise, Num 18:3–6 describes the needs of the Tabernacle:

> v. 3: "they shall attend [*weshameru*] to your needs [*mishmarteka*] and the needs [*umishmeret*] of all the Tabernacle."
>
> v. 4: "shall attend [*weshameru*] to the needs [*mishmeret*] of the Tabernacle of meeting for all the work [*abodat*] of the Tabernacle."
>
> v. 5: "and you shall attend [*ushemartem*] to the needs [*mishmeret*] of the sanctuary and the needs [*mishmeret*] of the altar."

Again, both humans and furnishing of the Tabernacle have needs (*mishmeret*) to be met. This language of *abad* and *shamar* for Tabernacle service, describes the meeting of the needs of humans and inanimate objects. These needs are met in the divine presence, and therefore by implication in the divine service.

This now brings us back to the nature of the service in the Garden. Ellen Davis reminds us that *abad* is usually service to someone or working the soil. The phrase "the work of the Tabernacle" (*abodat haohel*) refers to the work done in the Tabernacle by humans, but also appears to be inclusive of all that is done, including that done *by* the inanimate elements, in divine worship. The human and the inanimate work towards the same purpose of divine service. Davis argues that *abad* in Gen 2:15 means working for the needs of the soil, in the same way as I showed above that the Levites were to work for the needs of the Tabernacle and its furnishings. Care needs to be taken, she warns, for "biblical religion clearly forbids the divinization of the earth." Yet she takes worship as "to acknowledge worth," and hence the "soil is worthy of our service."[57] If the view I am advancing here is correct, the sense of *abad* here is that the Garden is valued and cared for so it might fulfil its divinely appointed function as sanctuary. The human serves the non-human to allow it to be fully itself.

---

57. Davis, *Scripture, Culture, and Agriculture*, 29.

Davis also recognizes that *shamar* means "keep," as related to flock, household, or brother, although ignores the obvious meaning of guard from Gen 3:24.[58] She also notes that the verb can also be translated as "observe." In Ps 107:43 we read that the one "who is wise give heed to (or observe, *weyishmar*) these things and they will understand the loving kindness of *Yhwh*." Here, *shamar* has the sense of reflect on, in this case on the deliverance of *Yhwh*, described as covenant love (*chesed*). In Hos 12:6, *shamar* is used in a moral sense, to "observe justice" (*shamar mishpat*). In Exod 31:13, the verb reflects observance of—i.e., obedience to—the command to keep the Sabbath. To *shamar* the Garden can therefore have polyvalent meaning. It clearly reflects a context of service to *Yhwh* in a sanctuary. Yet there is also the need to observe, learn from, and respect the limits of the Garden. Observation leads to obedience. This appears to be the sense of the conditional statement of Deut 4:40. The people were to keep (*weshamarta*) *Yhwh*'s statutes and commandments to live long on the *adamah*.[59]

The *adam* outside of the Garden

We have now seen that divine service in the Garden was both cultic and an exercise of kingly rule over the outside *adamah*. How then does the ejection from the Garden affect the relationship of the *adam* the *adamah*? For Wyatt, the relationship is broken.[60] He ties cultivation exclusively with the cult and hence, as the ejection from the Garden means a dethroning, this cultic gardening ceases. Does the activity of *abad* and *shamar* identified in Gen 2:15 cease in Gen 3:23–24? In v. 24 the cherubim now "guard" (*shamar*) the entrance to the garden. It is pure speculation as to whether the cherubim were present beforehand, and therefore it replaces the *adam* in this role. It is certainly an ironic reminder of failure to maintain the cult properly, and to *shamar* the Garden.

---

58. Davis, *Scripture, Culture, and Agriculture*, 30.
59. Davis, *Scripture, Culture, and Agriculture*, 30.
60. Wyatt, "Royal Garden," 25–26. Wyatt, "When Adam Delved," 117–22.

However, Wyatt's understanding seems at odds with Gen 3:23. *Yhwh* sends the *adam* and his wife out of the Garden to cultivate the soil (*leabod et haadamah*; Gen 3:23; cf. 2:5) from which the man was taken (*laqach*, Gen 3:19, 23; cf. 2:15). In fulfilment of Gen 2:5, the pair shall eat *eseb hasadeh* ("plants of the field"), although the *adamah* brings forth also thorns and thistles (Gen 3:18).[61] Wyatt suggests that the infinitive construct *leabod* is privative and not purposive; i.e., Gen 3:23 should read "to prevent him from tilling the ground from which he had been taken."[62] I find this unconvincing. There are 27 infinite constructions of *abad* in the Hebrew Bible, none of which appears to be privative. The only other occurrence of *leabod* in Genesis is found in 2:5, where it is clearly purposive. The example Wyatt gives of a privative case of a verb in 1 Kgs 4:24 contains a negating *lo* ("not"), so the construction is not analogous.[63]

Genesis 3:23 also contains a clue, combined with Gen 2:7–9, 15, that working the soil is an ongoing activity for the *adam*. Both the *adam* and the trees of the Garden are formed out of the *adamah*, but it is unclear from the narrative that it is the same *adamah*. Indeed, the *adam* is taken (*wayiqach*) by *Yhwh* and put *into* the Garden; i.e., removed from the *adamah* of his origin. In Gen 3:23, the *adam* is sent (*shalach*) out of the Garden (*gan*) to till the ground from which he had been taken (*laabod et haadamah asher luqach*). So, while kingship and cult appear to not function outside of the Garden (though see below), agriculture continues. Wyatt also suggests that *eseb hasadeh* in Gen 2:18 is best rendered vegetation of the steppe, and hence does not refer to agricultural produce but instead refers to a nomadic hunter-gatherer existence. This, however, contrasts with my earlier analysis of Gen 2:5–7, where

---

61. Stordalen argues that this vegetation is first supplied here since it is not mentioned previously. This is presumably because the *eseb hasadeh* are "cultured plants." Yet this assumes both that the *ed* does not fertilize the soil, but also likely ignores that fact that other humans lived outside of the Garden and that it was already suitable for their agricultural needs (Gen 4:14). Stordalen, "Man, Soil, Garden," 18.

62. Wyatt, "Royal Garden," 25. Wyatt, "When Adam Delved," 119.

63. Wyatt, "When Adam Delved," 119.

The Holy Garden

eseb hasadeh requires a cultivator, and hence refers to cultivated plants.

Wyatt's confusion seems to result from a failure to appreciate the role agriculture plays in the cult. In chapter 2, I noted that agricultural events are tied to events in Israel's salvation history (see Lev 23).[64] So, while Wyatt is likely correct that Gen 3:23 is a metaphor for "deportation and exile, implying the enforced cessation of the temple cult,"[65] the ongoing relationship of the *adam* to the *adamah* points in another direction; namely, that an ongoing relationship with *Yhwh* is possible outside of the Garden. Both Wyatt and Stordalen draw a hard line between life inside and outside of the Garden. Stordalen limits the blessings of Eden to the garden itself. While he admits that the luxury of Havilah possibly reflects the blessing from the river out of Eden via the Pishon, Stordalen understands the "explicit role of the rivers is to water the garden, whereafter the rest of the world more or less accidentally benefits."[66]

Yet Wyatt articulates the possibility of extending sacrality outside of the Garden. Four rivers extend out from a single source, suggests a world center approach to the Garden.[67] Hence, he states: "The point of the allusion to the Tigris and the Euphrates in a Jerusalem-centered text is surely to extend the sacrality of the latter, the place from which the Jews had been deported, to the place of their exile."[68] Such an understanding matches with the approach taken here, that there is an ongoing relationship with the *adamah* outside the Garden, and hence with *Yhwh*.

This ongoing relationship however is a troubled one, as we see with the story of Cain and Abel. Cain is described as a cultivator of the soil (*obed adamah*, Gen 4:2) in contrast to his brother who is a keeper of sheep.[69] There are strong resonances between

---

64. LeFebvre, *Liturgy of Creation*, 39.
65. Wyatt, "Royal Garden," 25.
66. Stordalen, "Man, Soil, Garden," 17.
67. Wyatt, "Royal Garden," 10.
68. Wyatt, "Royal Garden," 14.
69. It is unclear why Cain's offering from the ground (*adamah*) is rejected, but the text (Gen 4:7) hints at his motivations.

Cain's story and that of the Garden. Cain's fratricide was a failure to be his brother's keeper (*hashomer*, Gen 4:9), whereas the *adam* was meant "to till and to keep" (*leabedah uleshamerah*) the garden (Gen 2:15) and failed. Whereas the *adamah* was *arur* ("cursed") because the *adam* ate of the fruit (Gen 3:17), now Cain is *arur* because of his own actions, like the serpent (Gen 4:11; cf. 3:14). Just as *Yhwh* drove out (*garash*) *haadam* from the Garden (Gen 3:24), so Cain was driven out (*garash*) from the face of the ground (Gen 4:14). While east of Eden, *Yhwh* appears to have been present, but Cain would be hidden from *Yhwh*'s face. The drama of the soil and the human vocation worsens.

Cynthia Edenburg identifies structural parallels between the Garden story with the narrative of Cain: divine command (Gen 2:17; 3:1–5; cf. 4:6–7), its abrogation (3:6–7; cf. 4:8), denial of guilt (3:12, 13b; cf. 4:9), judgment (3:14–19; cf. 4:10–12), punishment via cursing the ground (3:17–19; cf. 4:11–12) so that it will not yield produce (3:18; cf. 4:12), care shown by the deity (3:21; cf. 4:13–15), expulsion (3:23–24; cf. 4:16) to east of Eden (3:24; cf. 4:16). The stories can be read as narratives of exile and alienation "for violating [God's] commandments and of failure to maintain essential social norms."[70] This pattern will be important later for understand the relationship between the non-P narratives and H in Leviticus 26.

Closer to the immediate literary context, however, Noah is a key to the restoration of order and the undoing of the cursing of the *adamah* (Gen 5:29; cf. 3:17–19). The name Noah (*Noach*) is derived from the root *nuach*, which means rest.[71] He was to provide comfort from toil (*itstsabon*, Gen 5:29; cf. 3:16–17). In Gen 8:21a, God does not continue to *leqalel haadamah* ("curse the earth") because of *haadam*.[72] The *adam*'s gloomy outlook on

---

70. Edenburg, "From Eden to Babylon," 156, 161–62. Harper, "*I Will Walk among You*," 205.

71. Longman et al., *Lost World of the Flood*, 116.

72. The word for curse (*qalal*) is stronger than that used in Lamech's declaration about Noah in Gen 5:29 (*arar*).

agriculture is lifted.[73] Theodore Hiebert notes that the response to Noah's burnt offerings in the Yahwist tradition is a listing of the major occasions in the agricultural year in the Israelite hill country (Gen 8:20–22).[74] Hence, there is an ongoing connection between agriculture and cult, one that goes back to the Garden itself, but is not restricted to it. However, even after Noah, the situation is still one of life outside of the Garden. Does the Hebrew Bible, in particular H, have any vision of a return to Eden?

Return to the Garden: The Edenization of Canaan

A return to Eden appears to be an aspect of the eschatology of the Hebrew Bible. This is apparent in two prophesies of restoration. Ezekiel 36:35 describes the restoration of the nation to the status of Eden:

> And they will say,
> "the earth [*haarets*] that was desolate
> has become as the Garden of Eden [*kegan eden*];
> and the waste and desolate and ruined towns
> are now inhabited and fortified."

The land (*haarets*) would be like the well-watered and fertile Garden (*gan*), just as empty cities would be filled with people and protected.[75] The possible parallel hints at the guarded nature of the Garden (Gen 2:15; 3:24). A similar prophesy is found in Isa 51:3:

> For *Yhwh* will comfort Zion;
> he will comfort all her waste places,
> and will make her wilderness as Eden [*keeden*],
> her desert as the garden of *Yhwh* [*kegan Yhwh*].

---

73. Zevit, *What Really Happened in the Garden of Eden?*, 223.

74. Hiebert, *Yahwist's Landscape*, 45–47.

75. Similar comparisons are also made in Ezekiel 47. See, for example, Stordalen, *Echoes of Eden*, 366–67.

Zion and her waste places which are wilderness and desert will be made like Eden, the Garden of *Yhwh*. Wyatt identified the Garden as a "synecdoche for the whole kingdom."[76]

This idea of Eden standing for the whole of Canaan has also been identified by Geoffrey Harper, in his study of the lexical relationships between Genesis 2–3, and H in Leviticus 26.[77] The key verb is *halak* (*hithpael mithalek*) "to walk about" (Gen 3:8). Harper observes that the use of the *hithpael* of *halak* with God as subject is only found seven times in the Hebrew Bible, and only twice outside of Gen 3:8 in the Pentateuch.[78] Wenham notes the use of this verb in elsewhere explicitly in the context of the Tabernacle.[79] Second Samuel 7:6–7 draws a contrast between God not dwelling in a house (*ki lo yashabti bebayith* v. 6) and moving about (walking, *halak*) within a tent and Tabernacle (*mithhalek beohel ubemishkan*, v. 6). This strongly suggests of "an analogous relationship" between tent/Tabernacle and the Garden.[80]

However, Wenham attempts to limit *Yhwh*'s walking solely to the Tabernacle (*mishkan*). In Deut 23:14, while the Tabernacle is clearly implied, the focus is on the camp (*machaneh*). *Yhwh* their God "walks in the midst of your camp" (*mithalek beqereb machaneka*). The specific purpose is defeat of Israel's enemies, conditional on the holiness of the camp (*machaneka qadosh*). While *Yhwh* dwells in the *ohel* ("tent") in Deuteronomy, Israel is not moving. Therefore, the divine walking in the camp implies the divine presence occupies the whole camp. The camp is to be holy, just as the sanctuary is holy.

Likewise, Wenham argues that the walking in Lev 26:12 referred specifically to the Tabernacle.[81] This is a possible reading if we take vv. 11 and 12 as a parallelism:

---

76. Wyatt, "Royal Garden," 17.
77. Harper, "*I Will Walk among You*," 194–98, 204–16.
78. Harper, "*I Will Walk among You*," 194.
79. Wenham, "Sanctuary Symbolism," 401.
80. Harper, "*I Will Walk among You*," 195.
81. Wenham, "Sanctuary Symbolism," 401.

v. 11a: "and I will set my Tabernacle among you."
v. 12a: "and I will walk [*wehithalakti*] among you."

Harper observes that while *Yhwh*'s walking in Gen 3:8 is in the context of impending judgment, in Lev 26:12 it comes as "the conclusion and climax of the blessings listed in vv. 4–12."[82] He further assumes that "walk among you" means just that—walk among the people beyond the confines of the Tabernacle; i.e., v. 11a is not a parallel to v. 12a. This is made clearer by considering the structure of the argument of the blessings in Lev 26:1–13. The section begins (v. 1) with three prohibitions, each beginning with the negative *lo*. The rationale for these prohibitions against idolatry is *ki ani Yhwh Elohim* ("for I am *Yhwh* your God"). Verse 2 is the counter command to keep the Sabbath and reverence the sanctuary, bringing together the protological temple and etiology of the Sabbath from Gen 1:1—2:3, as discussed in the previous chapter. This command has the same rationale as the prohibitions, albeit as the ellipsis *ani Yhwh* ("I am *Yhwh*"). Verse 3 is a conditional statement beginning with *im* ("if"). If the people obey, then the series of consecutive blessings, each beginning with the conjunction *waw* ("and"), follow. Verse 13 concludes with and explains the formula *ani Yhwh Elohim* ("I am *Yhwh* God") as the one who brought them out of slavery in Egypt. The cumulative argument from vv. 9–12 is one of increasing intimacy of *Yhwh* and his people:[83]

v. 9: "and I will confirm my covenant with you."
v. 11a: "and I will set my Tabernacle among you."
v. 11b: "and my soul will not abhor you."
v. 12a: "and I will walk among you."
v. 12b: "and be your God."
v. 12c: "and you shall be my people."

Hence the divine presence among the people is dependent on the existence of the sanctuary but, is not limited to it. *Yhwh* will walk among his people. This is also seen in the way in which Sabbath obedience is part of reverencing the temple, but is not limited to

---

82. Harper, *"I Will Walk among You,"* 194.
83. Harper, *"I Will Walk among You,"* 194.

it, at least for the laity (see chapter 2). As Milgrom notes: "*YHWH* is not confined to a sanctuary but is present everywhere in the land."[84] Or, as Harper observes: the passage presents a picture of "*YHWH* and the people of Israel cohabiting the same space."[85] This cohabitation is contingent on right walking by Israel (use of *halak* in Lev 26:3 in the positive, and negative in vv. 21, 23, 27, 40), lest *Yhwh* will walk hostilely or wrathfully (Lev 26:24, 28, 41).

This divine cohabitation with warnings of potential expulsion is consistent with structural parallels between Leviticus 26 and the Garden story. As noted earlier, Edenburg found parallels between the non-P narratives of Genesis 2–3 and 4 with a command, judgement, and expulsion structure. The expulsion included a cursing of the relationship with the *adam*, Cain, and the soil (*adamah*).[86] Harper demonstrates that Leviticus 26 also follows this structure.[87]

In his analysis, Lev 26:1–2 functions as a precis of the Decalogue, and represents the parallel to Gen 2:17, 3:1–5, and 4:8. The dual command to "keep" (*shamar*) the Sabbath and reverence the sanctuary echoes both H's integration of Genesis 1, as discussed in the last chapter, and the non-P Garden story. The result of disobedience includes making "your earth (*artsekem*) like bronze" (v. 19); i.e., making agriculture difficult, reminiscent of the curse on the *erets* because of the *adam* (Gen 3:17). This blight on the land includes a break in the supply of bread (*lechem*).[88] In Lev 26:5, covenant obedience leads to the people eating *lechem* to satisfaction, whereas in Lev 26:26, this supply is broken by covenant disobedience resulting in "and they shall dole out your bread (*lechem*) by weight; and though you eat (*waakaltem*), you shall not be satisfied". Harper observes that the combination *akal* ("eat") + *lechem* ("bread") as a divine pronouncement only occurs three times,

---

84. Milgrom, *Leviticus 23–27*, 2301.

85. Harper, "I Will Walk among You," 195.

86. Edenburg, "From Eden to Babylon," 157.

87. Harper, "I Will Walk among You," 204–5. Note this does not deny the Deuteronomist was aware of the Eden narrative. The same kind of choice presented in Leviticus 26 is evident in Deuteronomy 11. See Mettinger, *Eden Narrative*, 51.

88. Harper, "I Will Walk among You," 196.

together with the curse in Gen 3:19 of "by the sweat of your face you shall eat bread" (*bezeat apeka tokal lechem*).

Likewise, "the trees of the field shall yield their fruit" (*weets hasedah yiten piryow*, Lev 26:4) or "the trees of the land shall not yield their fruit" (*weets haarets lo niten piryow*, Lev 26:20), recalling the variety of fruiting trees in the Garden from which the pair could eat ("We may eat of the fruit of the trees in the garden" *miperi ets hagan nokel*, Gen 3:2–3). Finally, another significant lexical link between the Garden story and Leviticus 26 is that of wild animals (lit. "beast of the field," *chayat hasadeh*).[89] *Yhwh* brings them to the *adam* to name (Gen 2:19–20). In Lev 26:22, the *chayat hasadeh* will be one of *Yhwh*'s instruments of punishment.

In Gen 3:1, the serpent is also called is the craftiest of the *chayat hasadeh* and is cursed above all others for its role in "instigating the human insurgence against God" (Gen 3:15).[90] This suggests that the serpent figures as a kind of chaos monster, and that the failure of the *adam* was not guarding against chaos. Likewise, in Leviticus 26, disobedience to the covenant unleashes chaos, which includes the *chayat hasadeh*.

According to Priestly traditions, similarly, the consequences of covenant breaking will eventually lead to exile from the land. And one key aspect of covenant obedience is keeping the Sabbath (Lev 26:2), as argued in the previous chapter. In H (Lev 17–26), the holiness of the laity is stressed. Sabbath keeping was for all the people, but it was also for the land. The land has its own agency and requirement to "keep a Sabbath to *Yhwh*" (*weshabetah haarets shabat layhwh*, Lev 25:2). In Lev 26:35, the result of exile is that the land "shall have the rest (*tishbot*) it did not have on your sabbaths (*beshabetoteha*) when you were living on it." This implies that part of the reason for Israel's exile was that her Sabbath keeping did not benefit the *erets*. Land care in the form of proper Sabbath keeping is an expression of Israelite holiness, and now we can add one further element: the service of sacred earth is also a major theme in the second creation narrative.

---

89. Harper, "*I Will Walk among You*," 195.
90. Mettinger, *Eden Narrative*, 80–83.

Finally, I have shown that the entire *erets* can become a new Eden. This suggests that caring for the *erets* by granting its Sabbath rest can be linked to reverence for the sanctuary in a broader sense. The close link between Sabbath keeping and sanctuary reverencing extends both inward to the priestly functioning of the temple and outward to the agricultural and related practices of the laity.

We are now at a point where the exegetical fruits from the Priestly tradition, specifically the Holiness School's use of both Priestly and non-Priestly material, maybe applied to the problem of the Anthropocene. Recall, this new era of history is supported ideologically by capitalism and its emphasis on human mastery and control of nature. Progress is inevitable and the Anthropocene is an unfortunate stage in the development of human (capitalist) society. A marriage with some forms of Evangelical Christianity supports this, where the Anthropocene is the unavoidable outworking of divine judgment against humanity, but where this never appears to be against the sins of capitalism itself.

The exegesis of the previous two chapters demonstrates that for the Hebrews, Eden was sacred space, and that the land of Canaan was "Edenized." Reverencing the temple and keeping the Sabbath were central to Israelite holiness, and a way of keeping back the chaos that covenant disobedience brought. This included being rejected by the land they failed to provide proper rest for, being vomited out. Hence the Israelites had genuine agency in keeping chaos at bay by their weekly remembrance of the divine act of ordering. Further, the land was not a mere stage for a human-divine drama, but had agency to engage in its own unfolding, enjoy Sabbath rest, and vomit out the people. There are hints that in grounding the Sabbath etiology and the creation as sanctuary in creation and the general Semitic name for God, the Priestly imaginary allows for the potential Edenization of all creation.

In the final chapter, I will further explore these possibilities. Language of sanctuary and Sabbath offer the possibility of sacred space and time for human action to bring the world back from the brink of chaos. Likewise, fellow creatures become covenant partners.

4

The Ethical Anthropocene

An Ethical Challenge of the Anthropocene

THE ANTHROPOCENE REPRESENTS A departure from the relatively settled conditions of the Holocene that gave birth to agrarian civilization. This departure presents humanity with an existential threat. It also presents an ethical challenge, calling into the question an underpinning ideological driver of the Anthropocene, namely capitalism. As discussed in chapter 1, early capitalism's growth required two things. First, cheap labor, in the form of slaves, required the othering of non-Europeans. Secondly, the need for raw materials in the form of cheap nature led to settler colonialism with the Baconian narrative of "mastery over nature." The ongoing ecocidal destruction, displacement, and dispossession of the Anthropocene are a continuation of this narrative of mastery.

Two responses to the ethical problem of human mastery over nature invoke narratives of inevitability, in effect supporting Hamilton's point that many Holocene systems of belief are incapable of dealing with the rapidly changing conditions of the Anthropocene.[1] One secular view identifies the Anthropocene as an inevitable stage of human development.[2] Conservative Evangelicalism in general, and the marriage of American premillennial

---

1. Hamilton et al., *Anthropocene and the Global Environmental Crisis*, 5.
2. Frank, *Light of the Stars*, 208.

Evangelicalism with capitalism in particular, sees the Anthropocene as part of the unstoppable divine timetable, where it is unethical to intervene on behalf of those affected.[3] This thesis presents an alternative view, where human agency is a necessary part of the proper functioning of creation. In chapters 2 and 3, I examined the theology of the Priestly (P) creation account of Gen 1:1—2:3 and the non-P Garden story of Gen 2:5—3:34 respectively, together with their later development in the Holiness code (H) of Leviticus 17–26.

Three significant and interrelated themes emerge from that examination. The first concerns the notion of sanctuary and the creation of sacred space. In P's creation account, the earth is presented as a protological temple. This temple is completed after divine victory over the forces of chaos, but God is not enthroned until the construction of the Tabernacle (Exod 40). The prominent place given to chaos, and to the potential for human violence on the earth to release it, suggests that the narrative does not assume the Holocene quiescence that Clive Hamilton claims it does.[4] The Garden story presents Eden as the Jerusalem sanctuary. Both narratives present the Israelite vocation of tending for soil in the context of divine sovereignty and presence. In H, we see the potential for the "Edenization" of the land. In what follows, I explore the possibility of such Edenization.

The second main theme in our discussion has been the Sabbath and the creation of sacred time. H's reworking of P's creation account provides an etiological rationale for Sabbath keeping. The association of sanctuary and Sabbath is made clear in Lev 19:30, where Sabbath has cultic, economic, and ecological implications. Specifically, it can be argued that earth care is an aspect of Israelite holiness. This, as I will argue below, can be extended to Christian ethics in the Anthropocene.

A third theme concerns land and its role in both sacred space and time. P's account demonstrates that the earth participates in its own unfolding. The Garden story describes Israel's fundamental

---

3. Northcott, *Angel Directs the Storm*, 58–59.
4. Hamilton et al., *Anthropocene and the Global Environmental Crisis*, 5.

identification with and responsibility for the soil, in the office of sacral kingship. These themes are tied together in H, where the land is an active covenant partner. In what follows, I will argue that this provides a basis for an earth-centered ethic, both as the object of human ethical action, and as subject.

Sacred Space and the Sphere of Human Action

Chaos and Climate

The Primeval History presents God in combat with the forces of chaos. In comparison with other creation myths in Ancient Western Asia, the theme of combat is muted, but, nevertheless, creation is an incomplete project as chaos ever threatens. In Gen 1:2, the divine breath blows over the chaotic deep to subdue and order it. Parallels with the *Enuma Elish* identify the deep as the chaos monster Tiamat, and the sea monsters created on day five with her children. Chaos is an ongoing threat. The serpent (*nachash*, Gen 3:1) is one of the beasts of the field (*chayat hasadeh*), but also likely a chaos monster (*nachash* is also associated with the sea monster Leviathan in Isa 27:1). In P's Flood account, chaos in the form of the waters of the deep (*tehom*; Gen 7:11), is released in response to the violence filling the earth (Gen 6:13). The beasts of the field are presented as agents of chaos and judgment on Israel (Lev 26:22) for covenant breaches (Lev 26:1–2). The graphic imagery of the land vomiting out of the people in response to the defiling of the land (Lev 18:25–28) represents chaos, as the goodness of the land is undone (Lev 26:4, 26; cf. Gen 2:9).

Moving from the world of the biblical text to the Anthropocene requires a hermeneutical leap—a shift from P's cosmology and its relationship between human obedience and regular climate to a theologically informed scientific understanding. In scientific discourse, "chaos" has a different meaning related to the behavior of complex systems, such as the earth's climate.[5] Internal and external physical processes produce shifts between different states of

---

5. For an older popular introduction yet still useful, see Gleick, *Chaos*.

the climate. The Holocene represents an extended period where these processes have acted to maintain a stable climate amenable to human flourishing, yet even this may be in part due to human agency.[6] A departure from these stable conditions, which in turn disrupts human activity, may be viewed as chaos from a human, agrarian perspective, even when earth systems are obeying the "laws of nature."

The contrasting ideas of chaos in P and the modern world may be reconciled by considering the relationship between the law and the land. Northcott observes:

> From the Sabbath law the Hebrews adumbrated a range of related laws in the Deuteronomic code which moralised the material activities of agrarianism.[7]

This moralizing of agrarianism is also found in the Holiness Code, as we have seen.

One of the suggestions offered in chapters 2 and 3 was that the traditions of P and H understand creation to have a divinely-given agency. The earth embodies and carries out divine justice. This exegesis is consistent with work undertaken by Northcott, who demonstrates that in Jeremiah the neglect of the Sabbath is linked directly to the downfall of Jerusalem (Jer 17:27). Northcott unpacks the logic of this by considering, for example, Jeremiah 5. He sees a link between ecological disaster (v. 24) and destruction (vv. 15–17) with unfaithfulness to the laws and worship of *Yhwh*. The late Israelite monarchy and the merchant class placed "excessive ecological demands on the land."[8] There is a link between idolatry (v. 19), oppression of the poor (v. 28), and domination and destruction of ecosystems. So Northcott:

---

6. Bill Ruddiman has proposed that carbon dioxide emissions from land clearing associated with the beginnings of agriculture, and methane emissions from rice agriculture have helped keep the climate more temperate. See Ruddiman, *Plows, Plagues, and Petroleum*.

7. Northcott, *Moral Climate*, 11.

8. Northcott, *Moral Climate*, 11.

For the ancient Hebrews, justice was not a human invention but a divine attribute set into the character and structure of creation. When the people of God allowed their work on the land to displace the worship of God, and when they enslave one another and the land to serve the greed of the rich, the land lost its fertility and the rich and the poor alike were exiled from the land. The belief that justice is set into the creation order reflects a widespread assumption in the ancient world that biological and human communities are caught up in a nexus of relationships which also include heavenly bodies such as the sun, moon and stars, and the gods.[9]

Northcott's observations of the "nexus of relationships" echoes the views of Bińczyk and Chakrabarty, and the complexities of earth system modelling.[10] This nexus embodies the divine attribute of justice. Idolatry is worship of created things rather than the creator, including wealth and control. This leads to economic injustice, and eventually ecological collapse.[11]

My argument has at least three implications. First, as I will argue further below, creation care is an expression of Christian holiness and not, as in some forms of Evangelicalism, a distraction from it.[12] The Anthropocene points not to the eschatological schemes of premillennialism, but rather to divine goodness and human sinfulness.

A second implication is that "earth shattering" events are part of the Priestly imaginary. Exile was viewed as death, noting the dual meaning of dust (*aphar*) in Genesis 2–3, and was accompanied by struggles with creation (Gen 3:17–19). The forces of chaos are unleashed by human violence, and the regular order

---

9. Northcott, *Moral Climate*, 12.

10. Earth systems science examines the interactions between atmosphere, oceans, life, the solid earth, etc. See, for example, Lenton, *Earth System Science*.

11. Northcott, *Moral Climate*, 13.

12. It is also worth noting in passing, that creation care is more directly related to traditional concerns of mission and evangelism, due to the tight connection between natural law and divine law. The present ecological crisis is a manifestation both of human sinfulness and an indication of the divine law in nature.

of the world is turned upside down (Gen 7:11; cf. 1:2). To suggest, therefore, that the Holocene worldview of the Hebrews has no conception of human-caused catastrophe is an oversimplification of the texts examined here. Further, several aspects point towards both ongoing divine grace and human responsibility in the face of such events. As discussed in chapter 3, life outside of the garden/Jerusalem is still blessed by God as the four rivers go forth and bring life-giving water (Gen 2:10–14). Agricultural practice by the line of the *adam* indicates ongoing relationship with God outside of the land (Gen 4:1–7, 25–26). However, the goal was always return, for the possibility of restoration and return was available in response to repentance (Lev 26:40–45).

A third implication related to Northcott's work concerns the connection of relationships, understanding the agency and rights of creation. Especially for faith communities, the biblical literature can present a substantial challenge to Western dualisms. The evidence we have discussed is suggestive and has resonances in multiple directions.

Resources for Thinking about the Earth as Sacred

P's worldview provides one path that can contribute to the decolonizing of Christianity in countries like Australia. As Graham Paulson observes, Western Christianity has often understood the earth as adversary to be subdued (a misreading of Gen 1:26–28), resources for human use, or as a *terra nullius* to be divided up. For Aboriginal Christians to decolonize Christianity is to "pay respects to the spirituality that has long been attuned to the divine presences in this land," which is to recognize the "animistic spirituality" that has "shaped respectful attitudes to the created order."[13] Further work is required to establish whether the Priestly world is animistic in any meaningful sense, or is consistent with such a conception.[14]

---

13. Paulson, "Towards an Aboriginal Theology," 311.
14. See, for example, Joerstad, "Life of the World," ch. 3.

In Aotearoa New Zealand, for example, the Whanganui River has been granted the rights of a legal person.[15] Ecuador's constitution recognizes the rights of nature, while Bolivia recognizes the rights of "Mother Earth."[16] Whether or not Christians could recognize earth as "mother" in any meaningful way based on the Priestly imaginary or on Paul's writings is worth further examination.[17] What is suggestive is that the land in H has rights under the covenant with *Yhwh*. For these rights to be extended to cover the earth requires an understanding of the earth as sacred space, or even as—or *the*—icon of God.

The concept of the land of Canaan as Eden can be extended to include the earth via the kind of eschatology found in the Hebrew prophetic literature, as we have seen. Edenic language is also used eschatologically in Revelation 21–22 to encourage Christians suffering under the Roman Empire. As noted in chapter 3, Eden, when seen as the world's center, with four rivers radiating outwards, hints at divine blessing beyond the garden. In Rev 22:1–2, "Eden's tree of life has multiplied" and grows on both sides of the river (of Eden) and provides fruit all year.[18] The leaves are for the healing of the nations. Edenic language is also strongly invoked in the resurrection account in John 20.[19]

A second path for hermeneutical reflection is the political imaginary of P. Recall that P's creation account does not use the covenant name *Yhwh*, but rather the more general Semitic term *Elohim*. *Elohim*'s creation is of all of heaven and earth, which designates divine ownership. The enthronement is protological and completed in the construction of the Tabernacle (Exod 40), yet in P there is the trend towards inclusivity. As Mark Brett notes, there is a contrast between Gen 12:1–3, where it is *Yhwh* who promises to make Abram a "great nation" (*legow gadowl*), and Gen 17:1b–6,

---

15. See Boyd, *Rights of Nature*, ch. 8.

16. Boyd, *Rights of Nature*, chs. 10–11.

17. Paul states that creation is groaning in birth pains (*sunôdinô*). The tomb of the dust (*aphar*) becomes the womb of the resurrection.

18. Richter, *Stewards of Eden*, 103.

19. See Coloe, "Theological Reflections on Creation," 1–12.

where *El Shaddai* makes Abram a father of many "nations" (*goyim*). This echoes Exod 6:2–4 where *Yhwh* speaks to Moses to inform him he appeared as *El* to Moses' ancestors. From this, Brett draws the conclusion:

> Without any risk to later conceptions of monotheism, the Priestly theologian acknowledges a multiplicity of divine names and through them conveys a much more subtle account of divine sovereignty.[20]

What implications might this have for a conception of sacred earth, and with it for a human vocation to care for it? The first observation is that the Priestly discourse is genuinely inclusive. *Elohim* makes an eternal covenant (*berith olam*) with all creation (Gen 9:10, 16). All humans are made in the image of *Elohim* (Gen 1:26–27). Yet, as Brett notes, the political vocabulary of nations (*goyim*) is retained.[21] P's political imaginary contains "concentric circles constructed in hierarchical terms" with diversified vocabulary for God. The outer most circle contains all of creation, where God is known as *Elohim*. To Abraham's seed, God is known as *El Shaddai*. To Jacob-Israel in the land, God is known under the covenant name of *Yhwh*.[22] This sheds light on H's conception that both the Israelites and the nations are "bound by essentially the same ethical code," thus Israel risks too being vomited out by the land (Lev 18:24–25). Even the Israelites are viewed as immigrants (*gerim*) in the land, for *Yhwh* holds exclusive title (Lev 25:23).

This evidence affirms an inclusivity of people within the land, and the incumbent responsibility placed upon all to care for it. The fact that God is known by other names outside of the land, and that all the earth is included in an eternal covenant, hints strongly at an extension of sacredness, while retaining the centrality of the land. This imagery is retained in Revelation 21, where the kings of the earth bring their glory into the city (v. 24). Hence, care of one's land, whatever the name of God employed, is a sacred

---

20. Brett, *Political Trauma and Healing*, 93–94.
21. Brett, *Political Trauma and Healing*, 96.
22. Brett, *Political Trauma and Healing*, 99–100.

vocation. This implies a universal human responsibility for earth care, grounded in bearing the image of God. For the Christian, this image is reflected in the Triune nature of God; i.e., it is both monotheistic and christological. However, this does not deny the universality of the image of God, and hence the universality of the associated vocation.

Care of Sacred Earth

As argued above, care for the earth is in H an expression of Israelite holiness. By extension, earth care can also be an expression of Christian holiness for those who accept the Hebrew Bible as part of Scripture. Caring for the soil and proper worship are not separate activities. The former is part of the spectrum of the latter, from sanctuary to Sabbath. Such a recognition is an invitation to an agrarian hermeneutic, a theology of the soil. As Davis observes, land comes first.[23] One key aspect of the Anthropocene, the domination of the land by agricultural use and its attendant impacts on waterways and climate, is obscured by another, that of urbanization. Urban people need to be reminded that the bedrock of physical existence is food, and for civilization this means agriculture.[24] The witness of the Hebrew Bible is that justice is set into the structure of creation.[25]

As I argued in chapter 3, serving the needs of soil allows the earth to be fully what it is conceived to be, and that includes an inherent respect for the soil and its limits. Davis notes the ambiguity of the Hebrew *shamar* ("to keep"), as meaning also "observe," "learn from," and "respect" the limits of the Garden. A key observation of the task of the *adam* is that he "comes to Eden as a protector, answerable for the well-being of the precious thing that he did not make."[26] Soil is precious and takes a long time to form, while mod-

---

23. Davis, *Scripture, Culture, and Agriculture*, 28.
24. See Wirzba, *Food and Faith*.
25. Northcott, *Moral Climate*, 12.
26. Davis, *Scripture, Culture, and Agriculture*, 30–31.

ern agriculture has poisoned and squandered our topsoil.[27] Davis reminds us that the command "to keep" transcends simply agrarian techniques, and extends to an admission of human finitude and divine sovereignty. Humans have agency to care for soil, or to squander it, but to make soil is no simple task. As Davis further comments, such a reality challenges the idea that "human ingenuity runs up against physical limits only to overcome them."[28] What is required is not a wholesale rejection of the modern scientific method, but rather a rejection of the assumption "that we can accumulate enough knowledge to bend nature pliantly and to run the world."[29] What Davis then calls for is a "modest materialism" that is "concerned with ordering material existence in ways that are consonant with God's will and the design of the world." The former, God's will, is embedded in the latter. Ordering material existence in this way equates to worship in an Edenized world. The design of the world may include a rationality and agency independent of our own. Such a materialism bears little resemblance to the "materialistic scientism"[30] that seeks all its answers from scientific manipulation.

Conclusion: Sacred Time and the Care of Sacred Earth

In chapter 2, I argued that Sabbath keeping is a primary way of listening to and learning from both divine wisdom and the needs and limits of the earth. It is both an agrarian practice and rhythmic spirituality, weekly remembering the subduing of chaos. Sabbath underpins the timing for the other festivals of Israel (Lev 23). Keeping the Sabbath and revering the sanctuary are central to Israelite holiness (Lev 19:30, 26:2). Sabbath keeping was a sign to *Yhwh* that the people were fulfilling their part in the covenant.

---

27. Dotterweich, "History of Human-Induced Soil Erosion," 1–34.
28. Davis, *Scripture, Culture, and Agriculture*, 30.
29. Jackson, *Becoming Native to This Place*, 23.
30. Davis, *Scripture, Culture, and Agriculture*, 37.

In response, *Yhwh* would provide the seasonal rains to ensure the land would yield produce (Lev 26:3–5).

Without abrogating any sense of divine intervention into the earth's climate, the modern understanding of climate science indicates regular seasonal cycles with inter-seasonal variability. While H understands a simple logic of cause and effect—i.e., Sabbath keeping = seasonal rains—in climate science nothing is quite so simple. In the New Testament, rain and fruitful seasons are a sign of divine goodness (Acts 14:17), apparently unmerited goodness—especially in Matt 5:44–45, where the rain falls on the just and unjust alike. Returning to the Hebrew Bible's understanding of divine justice built into creation, we can see regular rains being more likely when the land is granted its Sabbath rest. For example, vegetation alters moisture and energy fluxes between the surface of the earth and the atmosphere. Deforestation in the Amazon rainforest negatively impacts regional rainfall.[31]

The Sabbath year (Lev 25:3–7) is fundamentally ecological, with a fallowing for the land essential in a pre-chemical fertilizer age.[32] The land rests but still produces food, without active management. Hence, LeFebvre concludes that, the "septennial land sabbath was an economic practice embodied within a theological institution."[33] The Jubilee year is a year of manumission of slaves and the return of ancestral land, and hence "provides a theological overlay for the social, economic reforms typically required with every generation for the sake of proper land management."[34] Sabbath then is fundamentally economic and ecological, humanitarian and environmental. Rather than being a mere passive ceasing from activity in the hope that God will act, an economy built on Sabbath ideals can be an active expression of human agency and responsibility. Sabbath can be understood as sound ecology, giving rest to agricultural land and natural ecosystems. It can form the

---

31. Spracklen and Garcia-Carreras, "Impact of Amazonian Deforestation," 9546–52.

32. LeFebvre, "Theology and Economics," 33.

33. LeFebvre, "Theology and Economics," 34.

34. LeFebvre, "Theology and Economics," 35.

basis of a more just economics, providing relief to the poor and returning ancestral lands. The fifty-year economic reset provides an active resistance to the tendency towards monopolies and concentration of resources that is a feature of capitalism.[35]

These features make Sabbath economics a potential theme for public theology, as well as an expression of Christian holiness. Some forms of Evangelical theology focus on issues of work or sport on the Sabbath. However, a more nuanced theology demonstrates that the Sabbath is centrally concerned about mercy and justice (Matt 12:1–8).

A close reading of Genesis 1–3 and the development of the key themes in the Holiness Code (Lev 17–26) reveals a potential basis for Christian ethics in the Anthropocene. Holocene regularity is not assumed in the pre-existent chaos that God brings under control; an instability in creation always threatens to be released as result of human violence. God creates sacred space, which eschatologically is to encompass the whole earth, and sacred time, which gives rest to human and non-human alike. Humans and non-humans actively participate in the unfolding of creation in covenant relationship with God, to fulfil their calling to worship. Such worship is not otherworldly but thoroughly ecological and economic.

---

35. On Sabbath economics, see Myers, *Biblical Vision of Sabbath Economics*.

Bibliography

Achenbach, Reinhard. "Sabbath in Genesis 1:1—2:3 and in the Pentateuch." In *Collected Essays on Creation and Temporality in Ancient Near Eastern and Biblical Texts*, edited by Sophie Ramond and Reinhard Achenbach, 18–32. Wiesbaden: Harrassowitz Verlag, 2019.

Ahhrenius, Svante. *Worlds in the Making: The Evolution of the Universe*. New York: Harper & Row, 1908.

Alberro, Heather. "Humanity and Nature Are Not Separate—We Must See Them as One to Fix the Climate Crisis." *The Conversation*, September 18, 2019. https://theconversation.com/humanity-and-nature-are-not-separate-we-must-see-them-as-one-to-fix-the-climate-crisis-122110.

Albertz, Rainer. "The Recent Discussion of the Formation of the Pentateuch/Hexateuch." *Hebrew Studies* 59 (2018) 65–92.

Almond, Philip C. "Five Aspects of Pentecostalism That Shed Light on Scott Morrison's Politics." *The Conversation*, May 23, 2019. https://theconversation.com/five-aspects-of-pentecostalism-that-shed-light-on-scott-morrisons-politics-117511.

Arnold, Bill. "Genesis 1 as Holiness Preamble." In *Let Us Go Up to Zion: Essays in Honour of H. G. M. Williamson on the Occasion of His Sixty-Fifth Birthday*, edited by Iain Provain and Mark J. Boda, 331–43. Leiden: Brill, 2012.

Artson, Bradley Shavit. "Vibrating over the Face of the Deep: God's Creating, and Ours." *CCAR Journal* 57 (2010) 40–47.

Averbeck, Richard E. "The Three 'Daughters' of Ba'al and Transformations of *Chaoskampf* in the Early Chapters of Genesis." In *Creation and Chaos: A Reconsideration of Hermann Gunkel's Chaoskampf Hypothesis*, edited by JoAnn Scurlock and Richard H. Beal, 237–56. Winona Lake: Eisenbrauns, 2013.

Barker, David C., and David H. Bearce. "End-Times Theology, the Shadow of the Future, and Public Resistance to Addressing Global Climate Change." *Political Research Quarterly* 66 (2013) 267–79.

Bar-On, Yinon M., et al. "The Biomass Distribution on Earth." *Proceedings of the National Academy of Science* 115 (2018) 6506–11.

Bibliography

Batto, Bernard. "The Image of God in the Priestly Creation Account." In *David and Zion: Biblical Studies in Honor of J. J. M. Roberts*, edited by Bernard F. Batto and Kathryn L. Roberts, 143–86. Winona Lake: Eisenbrauns, 2004.

Bauks, Michaela. "Sacred Trees in the Garden of Eden." *Journal of Ancient Judaism* 3 (2012) 267–301.

Bebbington, David W. *Evangelicalism in Modern Britain: A History from the 1730s to the 1980s*. London: Unwin Hyman, 1989.

Bińczyk, Ewa. "The Most Unique Discussion of the 21st Century? The Debate on the Anthropocene Pictured in Seven Points." *Anthropocene Review* 6 (2019) 3–18.

Bonneuil, Christophe, and Jean-Baptiste Fressoz. *The Shock of the Anthropocene*. London: Verso, 2016.

Boots, Bas, et al. "Effects of Microplastics in Soil Ecosystems: Above and Below Ground." *Environmental Science & Technology* 53 (2019) 1149–506.

Bostrom, Nick. "Where Are They? Why I Hope the Search for Extraterrestrial Life Finds Nothing." *MIT Technology Review* (2008) 72–77.

Boyd, David R. *The Rights of Nature: A Legal Revolution That Could Save the World*. Toronto: ECW, 2017.

Brett, Mark G. *Locations of God: Political Theology in the Hebrew Bible*. Oxford: Oxford University Press, 2019.

———. *Political Trauma and Healing: Biblical Ethics for a Postcolonial World*. Grand Rapids: Eerdmans, 2016.

Brueggemann, Walter. "From Dust to Kingship." *ZAW* 84 (1972) 1–18.

———. "The Kerygma of the Priestly Writers." In *The Vitality of Old Testament Traditions*, by Walter Brueggemann and Hans Walter Wolff, 101–14. Atlanta: Knox, 1982.

Carr, David. "Standing at the Edge of Reconstructable Transmission-History: Signs of a Secondary Sabbath-Oriented Stratum in Genesis 1:1—2:3." *VT* 70 (2020) 17–41.

Carr, Wylie, et al. "The Faithful Skeptics: Evangelical Religious Beliefs and Perceptions of Climate Change." *Journal for the Study of Religion, Nature, and Culture* 6 (2012) 276–99.

Carson, Rachel. *Silent Spring*. London: Penguin, 2001.

Chakrabarty, Dipesh. "Anthropocene Time." *History and Theory* 57 (2018) 5–32.

Chwałczyk, Franciszek. "Around the Anthropocene in Eighty Names—Considering the Urbanocene Proposition." *Sustainability* 12 (2020) 4458.

Coloe, Mary L. "Theological Reflections on Creation in the Gospel of John." *Pacifica* 24 (2011) 1–12.

Connolly, William E. "The Evangelical-Capitalist Resonance Machine." *Political Theory* 33 (2005) 869–86.

Crutzen, Paul. "Geology of Mankind." *Nature* 415 (2002) 23.

Davies, Anne. "Murray-Darling Basin Plan: Labor to Decide Whether It Will Back Key Changes." *Guardian*, May 7, 2018. https://www.theguardian.

com/australia-news/2018/may/07/murray-darling-basin-plan-labor-to-decide-whether-it-will-back-key-changes.

Davis, Ellen F. *Scripture, Culture, and Agriculture: An Agrarian Reading of the Bible*. Cambridge: Cambridge University Press: 2009.

Davis, Heather, and Zoe Todd. "On the Importance of a Date, or Decolonizing the Anthropocene." *ACME* 16 (2017) 761–80.

De Vos, Jurrian M., et al. "Estimating the Normal Background Rate of Species Extinction." *Conservation Biology* 29 (2014) 152–62.

Diamond, Jared. *Guns, Germs, and Steel*. London: Random House, 1998.

Dotterweich, Marcus. "The History of Human-Induced Soil Erosion: Geomorphic Legacies, Early Descriptions and Research, and the Development of Soil Conservation—A Global Synopsis." *Geomorphology* 201 (2013) 1–34.

Dozeman, Thomas B. *Exodus*. The Eerdmans Critical Commentary. Grand Rapids: Eerdmans, 2009.

Edenburg, Cynthia. "From Eden to Babylon: Reading Genesis 3–4 as a Paradigmatic Narrative." In *Pentateuch, Hexateuch, or Enneateuch? Identifying Literary Works in Genesis through Kings*, edited by Thomas B. Dozeman et al., 155–67. Atlanta: Society of Biblical Literature, 2011.

Enns, Peter. *The Evolution of Adam: What the Bible Does and Doesn't Say about Human Origins*. Grand Rapids: Brazos, 2012.

Environmental Pollution Panel, President's Science Advisory Committee. *Restoring the Quality of Our Environment*. Washington, DC: U.S. Government Printing Office, 1965.

Feinman, Peter. "An Analysis of Some of the Mesopotamian Motifs in Primeval J." In *Creation and Chaos: A Reconsideration of Hermann Gunkel's Chaoskampf Hypothesis*, edited by JoAnn Scurlock and Richard H. Beal, 172–89. Winona Lake: Eisenbrauns, 2013.

Frank, Adam. *Light of the Stars: Alien Worlds and the Fate of the Earth*. New York: Norton and Company, 2018.

Fretheim, Terrence E. "The Book of Genesis." In *The New Interpreter's Bible*. Vol. 1, *Genesis to Leviticus*, edited by Leander E. Keck, 17–276. Nashville: Abingdon, 1994.

———. *God and World in the Old Testament: A Relational Theology of Creation*. Nashville: Abingdon, 2005.

Friedrich, Tobias, et al. "Detecting Regional Anthropogenic Trends in Ocean Acidification against Natural Variability." *Nature Climate Change* 2 (2012) 167–71.

Fukuyama, Francis. "The End of History." *National Interest* 16 (1989) 3–18.

Fuller, Errol. *Dodo: From Extinction to Icon*. New York: Collins, 2002.

Funk, Cary, and Becka A. Alper. *Religion and Science: Highly Religious Americans Are Less Likely Than Others to See Conflict between Faith and Science*. Washington: Pew Research Centre, 2015.

Gaffney, Owen, and Will Steffen. "The Anthropocene Equation." *Anthropocene Review* 4 (2017) 53–61.

Bibliography

Gleeson-White, Jane. *Six Capitals: Capitalism, Climate Change, and the Accounting Revolution That Can Save the Planet.* Sydney: Allen and Unwin, 2020.

Gleick, James. *Chaos: Making a New Science.* New York: Viking, 1987.

Goldberg, Matthew H., et al. "Social Identity Approach to Engaging Christians in the Issue of Climate Change." *Science Communication* 41(2019) 442–63.

Habel, Norman. *An Inconvenient Text: Is a Green Reading of the Bible Possible?* Adelaide: ATF, 2009.

Hall, Shannon. "Exxon Knew about Climate Change Almost 40 Years Ago." *Scientific American*, October 26, 2018. https://www.scientificamerican.com/article/exxon-knew-about-climate-change-almost-40-years-ago/.

Hamilton, Clive. *Scorcher: The Dirty Politics of Climate Change.* Melbourne: Black, 2007.

Hamilton, Clive, et al., eds. *The Anthropocene and the Global Environmental Crisis: Rethinking Modernity in a New Epoch.* London: Routledge, 2015.

Hansen, James, et al. "Target Atmospheric CO_2: Where Should Humanity Aim?" *Open Atmospheric Science Journal* 2 (2008) 217–31.

Harper, G. Geoffrey. *"I Will Walk among You": The Rhetorical Function of Allusions to Genesis 1–3 in the Book of Leviticus.* University Park: Eisenbrauns, 2018.

Harrison, Peter. "'Fill the Earth and Subdue It': Biblical Warrants for Colonization in Seventeenth Century England." *Journal of Religious History* 29 (2005) 3–24.

Heidel, Alexander. *The Babylonian Genesis: The Story of Creation.* Chicago: University of Chicago Press, 1963.

Heiser, Michael. "Monotheism, Polytheism, Monolatry, or Henotheism? Toward an Assessment of Divine Plurality in the Hebrew Bible." *Bulletin for Biblical Research* 18 (2008) 1–30.

Hendel, Ronald S. *The Text of Genesis 1–11: Textual Studies and Critical Edition.* Oxford: Oxford University Press, 1998.

Hendon, Harry H., et al. "Seasonal Variations of Subtropical Precipitation Associated with the Southern Annular Mode." *Journal of Climate* 27 (2014) 3446–60.

Hiebert, Theodore. *The Yahwist's Landscape Nature and Religion in Early Israel.* Oxford: Oxford University Press, 1996.

Hughes, Brent B., et al. "Climate Mediates Hypoxic Stress on Fish Diversity and Nursery Function at the Land-Sea Interface." *Proceedings of the National Academic of Science* 112 (2015) 8025–30.

International Union of Geological Scientists. "International Chronostratigraphic Chart." https://www.iugs.org/ics.

IPCC. "Summary for Policymakers." In *Climate Change and Land: An IPCC Special Report on Climate Change, Desertification, Land Degradation, Sustainable Land Management, Food Security, and Greenhouse Gas Fluxes in Terrestrial Ecosystems*, edited by P. R. Shukla et al. Cambridge: Cambridge University Press, 2022.

Bibliography

Irving-Stonebraker, Sarah. "From Eden to Savagery and Civilization: British Colonialism and Humanity in the Development of Natural History, ca. 1600–1840." *History of the Human Sciences* 32 (2019) 63–79.

Jackson, Robert B., et al. "The Depths of Hydraulic Fracturing and Accompanying Water Use across the United States." *Environmental Science & Technology* 49 (2015) 8969–76.

Jackson, Wes. *Becoming Native to this Place*. Lexington: University Press of Kentucky, 1994.

Jennings, Willie. *The Christian Imagination: Theology and the Origins of Race*. New Haven: Yale University Press, 2011.

Jess, Allison. "DDT Environmental Effects." *ABC Goulburn Murray*, October 11, 2007. http://www.abc.net.au/local/stories/2007/10/09/2054547.htm.

Joerstad, Mari. "The Life of the World: The Vitality and Personhood of Non-animal Nature in the Hebrew Bible." PhD diss., Duke University, 2016.

Joosten, Jan. *People and the Land in the Holiness Code: An Exegetical Study of the Ideational Framework of the Law in Leviticus 17–26*. Leiden: Brill, 1996.

Judd, Bridget, and Catherine Taylor. "Smoke and Bushfires Are the New Norm, So How Do We Beat the 'Airpocalypse.'" *ABC News*, December 7, 2019. https://www.abc.net.au/news/2019-12-07/nsw-fire-smoke-air-pollution-how-our-lives-will-need-to-change/11761098.

Kahane, Guy. "Mastery without Mystery: Why There Is No Promethean Sin in Enhancement." *Journal of Applied Philosophy* 28 (2011) 355–68.

Keller, Catherine. *Face of the Deep: A Theology of Becoming*. New York: Routledge, 2003.

Kempf, Stephen. "Introducing the Garden of Eden: The Structure and Function of Genesis 2:4B–7." *Journal of Translation and Textlinguistics* 7 (1996) 33–53.

Kidner, Derek. "Genesis 2:5, 6: Wet or Dry?" *Tyndale Bulletin* 17 (1966) 109–14.

Knohl, Israel. *The Sanctuary of Silence: The Priestly Torah and the Holiness Code*. Minneapolis: Fortress, 1995.

Kolbert, Elizabeth. *The Sixth Extinction: An Unnatural History*. New York: Holt and Company, 2014.

Krüger, Thomas. "Genesis 1:1—2:3 and the Development of the Pentateuch." In *The Pentateuch: International Perspectives on Current Research*, edited by Thomas B. Dozeman et al., 125–38. Tübingen: Mohr Siebeck, 2011.

LeFebvre, Michael. "Adam Reigns in Eden: Genesis and the Origins of Kingship." *Bulletin of Ecclesial Theology* 5 (2018) 25–57.

———. *The Liturgy of Creation: Understanding Calendars in Old Testament Context*. Downers Grove: InterVarsity, 2019.

———. "Theology and Economics in the Biblical Year of Jubilee." *BET* 2 (2015) 31–51.

Lenton, Tim. *Earth System Science: A Very Short Introduction*. Oxford: Oxford University Press, 2016.

Levenson, Jon D. *Creation and the Persistence of Evil: The Jewish Drama of Divine Omnipotence*. Princeton: Princeton University Press, 1988.

BIBLIOGRAPHY

Lewis, Simon L., and Mark A. Maslin. "Defining the Anthropocene." *Nature* 519 (2015) 171–80.

———. *The Human Planet: How We Created the Anthropocene*. London: Pelican, 2018.

Lindenau, J. D., et al. "Distribution Patterns of Variability for 18 Immune System Genes in Amerindians—Relationship with History and Epidemiology." *Tissue Antigens* 82 (2013) 177–85.

Liu, Xuejun, et al. "Enhanced Nitrogen Deposition over China." *Nature* 494 (2013) 459–62.

Longman, Tremper, et al. *The Lost World of the Flood*. Grand Rapids: IVP Academic, 2018.

Maslin, Mark. "Forty Years of Linking Orbits to Ice Ages." *Nature* 540 (2016) 208–9.

McBrien, Justin. "Accumulating Extinction: Planetary Catastrophism in the Necrocene." In *Anthropocene or Capitalocene? Nature, History, and the Crisis of Capitalism*, edited by Jason W. Moore, 116–37. Oakland: PM, 2016.

McGrath, Alister E. *The Reenchantment of Nature: Science, Religion, and the Human Sense of Wonder*. London: Hodder and Stoughton, 2002.

Mettinger, Tryggve N. D. *The Eden Narrative: A Literary and Religio-Historical Study of Genesis 2–3*. Winona Lake: Eisenbrauns, 2007.

Millard, A. R. "The Etymology of Eden." *Vetus Testamentum* 36 (1984) 104–5.

Milgrom, Jacob. *Leviticus 23–27: A New Translation with Introduction and Commentary*. Anchor Bible 3B. New Haven: Yale University Press, 2007.

Mobley, Gregory. *The Return of the Chaos Monsters—And Other Backstories of the Bible*. Grand Rapids: Eerdmans, 2012.

Moltmann, Jürgen. *Science and Wisdom*. Translated by Margaret Kohl. Minneapolis: Fortress, 2009.

Montoya, José M., et al. "Why a Planetary Boundary, If It Is Not Planetary, and the Boundary Is Undefined? A Reply to Rockström et al." *Trends in Ecology & Evolution* 33 (2018) 234.

Moore, Jason W., ed. *Anthropocene or Capitalocene? Nature, History, and the Crisis of Capitalism*. Oakland: PM, 2016.

———. "The Rise of Cheap Nature." In *Anthropocene or Capitalocene? Nature, History, and the Crisis of Capitalism*, edited by Jason W. Moore, 78–115. Oakland: PM, 2016.

Morgan, Jonathan. "Transgressing, Puking, Covenanting: The Character of Land in Leviticus." *Theology* 112 (2009) 173–80.

Morton, Timothy. *Being Ecological*. Milton Keynes: Pelican, 2018.

Muschitiello, Francesco, et al. "Deep-Water Circulation Changes Lead North Atlantic Climate During Deglaciation." *Nature Communications* 10 (2019) https://doi.org/10.1038/s41467-019-09237-3.

Myers, Ched. *The Biblical Vision of Sabbath Economics*. Washington: Church of the Saviour, 2001.

BIBLIOGRAPHY

Nagaoka, Lisa, et al. "The Overkill Model and Its Impact on Environmental Research." *Ecology and Evolution* 8 (2018) 9683–96.

NASA Goddard Space Flight Centre. "NASA Ozone Watch." https://ozonewatch.gsfc.nasa.gov/.

NOAA Global Monitoring Laboratory. "Trends in Atmospheric Carbon Dioxide." https://www.esrl.noaa.gov/gmd/ccgg/trends/.

Northcott, Michael. *An Angel Directs the Storm: Apocalyptic Religion & American Empire*. London: Taurus, 2004.

———. *A Moral Climate*. Maryknoll, NY: Orbis, 2007.

Oßmann, Barbara E. "Microplastics in Drinking Water? Present State of Knowledge and Open Questions." *Current Opinion in Food Science* 41 (2021) 44–51.

Oreskes, Naomi, and Erik M. Conway. *Merchants of Doubt: How a Handful of Scientists Obscured the Truth on Issues from Tobacco Smoke to Global Warming*. London: Bloomsbury, 2011.

Paulson, Graham. "Towards an Aboriginal Theology." *Pacifica* 19 (2006) 310–20.

Pepper, Miriam, and Rosemary Leonard. "How Ecotheological Beliefs Vary among Australian Churchgoers and Consequences for Environmental Attitudes and Behaviors." *Reviews of Religious Research* 58 (2016) 101–24.

Pope, Mick. "The Sea Is Eating the Ground: A Theology of Sea Level Rise." *Anglican Theological Review* 100 (2018) 79–92.

Rad, Mani Rouhi, et al. "Downside Risk of Aquifer Depletion." *Irrigation Science* 38 (2020) 577–91.

Ramantwana, Hulisani. "Humanity Not Pronounced Good: A Re-reading of Genesis 1:26–31 in Dialogue with Genesis 2–3." *Old Testament Essays* 26 (2013) 425–44.

Rhyder, Julia. "Sabbath and Sanctuary Cult in the Holiness Legislation: A Reassessment." *JBL* 138 (2019) 721–40.

Richter, Sandra L. *Stewards of Eden: What Scripture Says about the Environment and Why It Matters*. Downers Grove: InterVarsity, 2020.

Rogland, Max. "Interpreting אד in Genesis 2.5–6: Neglected Rabbinic and Intertextual Evidence." *JSOT* 34 (2010) 379–93.

Römer, Thomas. "The Elusive Yahwist: A Short History of Research." In *A Farewell to the Yahwist? The Composition of the Pentateuch in Recent European Interpretation*, edited by Thomas B. Deozeman and Konrad Schmidt, 9–27. Atlanta: Society for Biblical Literature, 2006.

———. "The Problem of the Hexateuch." In *The Formation of the Pentateuch: Bridging the Academic Cultures of Europe, Israel, and North America*, edited by Jan C. Gertz et al., 813–27. Tübingen: Mohr Siebeck, 2016.

Ruddiman, William F. *Plows, Plagues, and Petroleum: How Humans Took Control of Climate*. Princeton: Princeton University Press, 2016.

Sachs, Jeffrey. "How the AEI Distorts the Climate Debate." *Huffpost*, August 2, 2014, updated December 6, 2017. https://www.huffingtonpost.com/jeffrey-sachs/how-the-aei-distorts-the_b_4751680.html.

Bibliography

Sample, Ian. "Scientists Offered Cash to Dispute Climate Study." *Guardian*, February 3, 2007. https://www.theguardian.com/environment/2007/feb/02/frontpagenews.climatechange.

Savoca, Matthew S., et al. "Marine Plastic Debris Emits a Keystone Infochemical for Olfactory Foraging Seabirds." *Science Advances* 2 (2016) e1600395.

Schmidt, Jeremy J., et al. "Ethics in the Anthropocene: A Research Agenda." *Anthropocene Review* 3 (2016) 188–200.

Schmid, Konrad. "The Quest for 'God': Monotheistic Arguments in the Priestly Texts of the Hebrew Bible." In *Reconsidering the Concept of Revolutionary Monotheism*, edited by B. Pongratz-Leisten, 271–89. Winona Lake: Eisenbrauns, 2011.

Schwartz, Sarah. "Narrative *Toledot* Formulae in Genesis: The Case of Heaven and Earth, Noah, and Isaac." *Journal of Hebrew Scriptures* 16 (2016). https://doi.org/10.5508/jhs.2016.v16.a8.

Siddique, Shabana, et al. "Air Pollution and Its Impact on Lung Function of Children in Delhi, the Capital City of India." *Water, Air, & Soil Pollution* 212 (2015) 89–100.

Simkin, Ronald A. "Creation and Theodicy in the Context of Climate Change: A New Cosmology for the Anthropocene?" *Journal of Religion and Society Supplement Series* 18 (2019) 237–39.

Simon, Zoltán Boldizsár. "Why the Anthropocene Has No History: Facing the Unprecedented." *Anthropocene Review* 4 (2017) 239–45.

Slezak, Michael, and Anne Davies. "Murray-Darling Water Theft Allegations: NSW to Prosecute Irrigators." *Guardian*, March 8, 2018. https://www.theguardian.com/australia-news/2018/mar/08/murray-darling-water-theft-allegations-nsw-to-prosecute-irrigators.

Solomon, Susan, et al. "Emergence of Healing in the Antarctic Ozone Layer." *Science* 353 (2016) 269–74.

Spracklen, D. V., and L. Garcia-Carreras. "The Impact of Amazonian Deforestation on Amazon Basin Rainfall." *Geophysical Research Letters* 42 (2015) 9546–52.

Staal, Arie, et al. "Hysteresis of Tropical Forests in the 21st Century." *Nature Communications* 11 (2020) 1–8. https://doi.org/10.1038/s41467-020-18728-7.

Stackert, Jeffrey. "Compositional Strata in the Priestly Sabbath: Exodus 31:12–17 and 35:1–3." *Journal of Hebrew Scriptures* 11 (2011). https://doi.org/10.5508/jhs.2011.v11.a15.

———. "Holiness Code and Writings." In *The Oxford Encyclopedia of the Bible and Law*. Vol. 1, *ADM–LIT*, edited by Brent A. Strawn, 389–96. Oxford: Oxford University Press, 2015.

———. "The Sabbath of the Land in the Holiness Legislation: Combining Priestly and Non-priestly Perspectives." *Catholic Biblical Quarterly* 73 (2011) 239–50.

Steffen, Will, et al. "The Trajectory of the Anthropocene: The Great Acceleration." *Anthropocene Review* 2 (2015) 1–18.

BIBLIOGRAPHY

Steffen, Will, et al. "Planetary Boundaries: Guiding Human Development on a Changing Planet." *Science* 347 (2015). DOI: 10.1126/science.1259855.

Steffen, Will, et al. "Trajectories of the Earth System in the Anthropocene." *Proceedings of the National Academic of Science* 115 (2018) 8252–59.

Stordalen, Terje. *Echoes of Eden: Genesis 2–3 and the Eden Garden in Biblical Hebrew Literature*. Leuven: Peeters, 2000.

———. "Genesis 2,4: Restudying a *Locus Classicus*." *ZAW* 104 (1992) 163–77.

———. "Man, Soil, Garden: Basic Plot in Genesis 2–3 Reconsidered." *JSOT* 53 (1992) 3–26.

Szaj, Patryk. "Hermeneutics at the Time of the Anthropocene: The Case of Hans-Georg Gadamer." *Environmental Values* 30 (2021) 235–54.

Thompson, Philip E. S. "The Yahwist Creation Story." *VT* 21 (1971) 197–208.

Tsumura, David. *Creation and Destruction: A Reassessment of the ChaosKampf in the Old Testament*. Winona Lake: Eisenbrauns, 2005.

Wallace, John M., and Peter V. Hobbs. *Atmospheric Science*. 2nd ed. Amsterdam: Academic, 2006.

Walton, John. *The Lost World of Genesis One: Ancient Cosmology and the Origins Debate*. Downers Grove: InterVarsity, 2009.

Ward, Kate. "Wealthy Hyperagency in a Throwaway Culture: Inequality and Environmental Death." In *Integral Ecology for a More Sustainable World: Dialogues with "Laudato Si'*," edited by Dennis O'Hara et al., 77–90. Lanham: Lexington, 2020.

Weinfeld, Moshe. "Sabbath, Temple, and the Enthronement of the Lord—The Problem of the Sitz im Leben of Genesis 1:1—2:3." In *Mélanges bibliques et orientaux en l'honneur de M. Henrie Cazelles*, edited by A. Caquot and M. Delcor, 501–12. Kevelaer: Butzon & Bercker, 1981.

Welker, Michael. *Creation and Reality*. Minneapolis: Ausburg Fortress, 1999.

Wenham, Gordon J. "Sanctuary Symbolism in the Garden of Eden Story." In *"I Studied Inscriptions from before the Flood": Ancient Near Eastern, Literary, and Linguistic Approaches to Genesis 1–11*, edited by Richard S. Hess, 399–404. Winona Lake: Eisenbrauns, 1994.

Westaway, Michael C., et al. "At Least 17,000 Years of Coexistence: Modern Humans and Megafauna at the Willandra Lakes, South-Eastern Australia." *Quaternary Science Reviews* 157 (2017) 206–11.

Whelan, Robert, et al. *The Cross and the Rain Forest: A Critique of Radical Green Spirituality*. Grand Rapids: Eerdmans, 1996.

White, Lynn, Jr. "The Historical Roots of Our Ecologic Crisis." *Science* 155 (1967) 1203–7.

Wirzba, Norman. *Food and Faith: A Theology of Eating*. Cambridge: Cambridge University Press, 2011.

Wright, David P. "Holiness in Leviticus and Beyond: Different Perspectives." *Interpretation* 53 (1999) 351–64.

Wyatt, Nicholas. "A Royal Garden: The Ideology of Eden." *Scandinavian Journal of the Old Testament* 28 (2014) 1–35.

BIBLIOGRAPHY

———. "When Adam Delved: The Meaning of Genesis III 23." *VT* 38 (1988) 117–22.

Zevit, Ziony. *What Really Happened in the Garden of Eden?* New Haven: Yale University Press, 2013.

Name Index

Achenbach, Reinhard, 34
Arrhenius, Svante, 13
Arnold, Bill, 28n18
Averbeck, Richard, 39

Barker, David, 18
Batto, Bernard, 40
Bauks, Michaela, 69
Bearce, David, 18
Bebbington, David, 16
Bińczyk, Ewa 15, 89
Bostrom, Nick, 12
Brett, Mark, 27, 91–92
Brueggemann, Walter, 70, 71n50, 72

Carr, David, 33–34, 38
Carr, Wylie, 16, 18–19
Carson, Rachel, 4
Chakrabarty, Dipesh, 14–15, 89
Connolly, William, 20
Conway, Erik, 13
Crutzen, Paul, 1, 10

Davis, Ellen, 43n62, 74–75, 93–94

Edenburg, Cynthia, 78, 82

Feinman, Peter, 66–67
Frank, Adam, 11–12

Fretheim, Terrence, 26n11, 44

Gaffney, Owen, 7
Goldberg, Mathew, 17

Habel, Norman, 26, 56
Hamilton, Clive, xi, 13, 16, 85–86
Harper, Geoffrey, 80–82
Hendel, Ronald, 30–32

Israel, Kohl, 28n19

Joerstad, Mari, 50

Kempf, Stephen, 58n7, 59
Krüger, Thomas, 34

LeFebvre, Michael, 44, 95
Leonard, Rosemary, 20–21
Levenson, Jon, 35, 37–39, 42, 45, 48–49
Lewis, Simon, 10

Maslin, Mark, 8, 10
McBrien, Justin 15
Milgrom, Jacob, 82
Moore, Jason, 14

Northcott, Michael, 18–20, 88–89

Name Index

Oreskes, Naomi, 13

Pepper, Miriam, 20–21

Rhyder, Julia, 45, 47, 49
Rogland, Max, 64
Ruddiman, William, 9

Schmidt, Jeremy, xi
Schmidt, Konrad, 37
Simkin, Ronald, 26
Stackert, Jeffrey, 47n73, 52
Steffen, Will, 7
Stordalen, Terje, 59–60, 64–65,
    76n61, 77

Tsumura, David, 39

Walton, John, 42–43
Welker, Michael, 50
Wenham, Gordon, 68–69, 80
White, Lynn, 24
Wyatt, Nicholas, 56, 67–68,
    75–77, 80

Subject Index

Adam(ah), 83
    gardener, 72–74
    image bearer, 51, 60
    king, 23, 66, 70–71
    relationship to soil, 57–58,
        61–64, 75–78, 82, 90, 93
agency
    human, xi, 7, 14–15, 18, 20,
        22, 50, 86, 88, 94–95
    non-human creation, xiii,
        14–15, 23, 29, 50, 53, 60,
        83–84, 88, 90, 94
agriculture, 1, 5, 9, 23, 28n19,
    42–44, 51, 76–79, 82
    88n6, 93–94
agricultural, 5, 42–47, 52, 54,
    61, 63, 72, 76–79, 84, 90,
    93, 95
Anthropocene, xi, xiii, 1–2,
    6–16, 20, 22–27, 45, 50,
    55–56, 84–89, 93, 96
aphar, 62–65, 70–72, 89, 91n17

Canaan, xii, 23, 26n9, 30, 57, 67,
    80, 84, 91
Capitalism, xiii, 13–22, 24,
    84–86, 96
Capitalocene, 14–16
chaos, viii, xii–xiii, 22–23, 27–
    30, 34–35, 37–38, 42–49,
    51–54, 83–84, 86–89,
    94, 96

Chaoskampf, xii, 22, 29, 35, 39,
    54
climate, 1–2, 6, 9, 21n102,
    87–88, 93, 95
    change, vii, 2, 5, 13, 15–19
    scepticism, 16, 21n102
civilization, 1, 11–12, 85, 93
colonialism, 14n65, 15, 85
command, 26n11, 46, 50, 54, 57,
    75, 78, 81–82, 94
    commandment(s), 46, 48,
        75, 78
creation
    Adam, 57–58, 61, 65–66,
        70–72
    agriculture, 42–45
    care, 17
    combat, 36–41
    human rule, 21
    justice, 93, 95
    non-human, 25n3, 27
    ordering of, 35
    Sabbath, 46, 49–55
    temple, 22, 41, 45

day(s), 13, 28n18, 31–34, 36,
    38–39, 42–47, 54, 58–60,
    87
    of judgement, 20
    Sabbath, 33
    seventh, xii–xiii, 32–34,
        41–42, 46–47, 54

Subject Index

dust, 57, 58n6, 62–66, 70–71, 72n50, 89, 91n17

Earth, xiii, 7, 14–20, 23, 28n18, 29, 31, 36–41, 43n62, 48, 51, 55–67, 70, 74, 78–79, 82–83, 86–96
   agency, xiii, 23, 86
   care, xii, 26, 56–57, 86–87, 93
   Edenizing, xii
   and heavens, 33, 36, 51, 58n7, 59–60, 65, 67
   new, 19
   as sacred, 83, 86, 91–92, 96
   system, xi, 2, 4, 7, 11–12, 14, 88–89
Elohim, 31–41, 46, 56n2, 57n7, 59–61, 68, 81, 91–92
Enuma Elish, 35–40, 58, 87
environmental, vii, xi, xiii, 6, 13n62, 17–22, 25, 95
erets, xiii, 31, 40, 44, 49–51, 55, 58n7, 59–66, 82–84
ethics, xi, 86, 96
Evangelical, 16, 18, 20–22, 84, 96
Evangelicalism, 16, 20, 24, 85–86, 89
evangelism, 16, 18–19, 89n20
exile, 23, 28n19, 30, 53, 57, 71, 77–78, 83, 89
exilic, 26n11, 45–46
extinction, 3–5, 8, 14

Flood, xii–xiii, 17, 22, 29, 35, 40, 44, 48, 87
food, 3, 9, 36, 42–43, 49, 62, 73, 93, 95

Garden of Eden, 18
   Adam as gardener of, 23, 57, 66, 70–75
   ejection as exile, 57

genealogy, 61–65
   life outside, 75-79, 90–91
   location, xii, 67–69
   return to, 79–86
   story of, 58–60
generation/s, 27, 59–60, 63, 66, 95
Great Acceleration, 1, 7, 10–11
ground, 43, 61–65, 70–73, 76–78

heptad(ic), 22, 28n18, 29–33, 39, 42, 58n7
history, viii, 20, 23, 44–45, 77, 84
   geological, xi, 3n12, 11, 14
   human, xi, 19
   Pentateuch, 27, 34
   Primeval, xii, 22, 56n2, 57, 59–61, 87
Holiness
   Christian, 89, 93, 96
   Code, School, xii–xiii, 22, 28–29, 45, 54–55, 57, 84, 86, 88, 96
   God, 46, 48
   Israel, viii, xiii, 23, 29, 46–48, 55, 57, 80, 83–84, 86, 93–94
Holocene, 1–2, 7, 9, 16, 20, 85–86, 88, 90, 96
humanity, xi, 12, 14, 20–21, 25n3, 55, 84–85

industrial, 4, 6, 20
   Pre-, 3, 7
   Revolution, 1, 3, 10
king, 23, 66, 68, 71–73
kingly, 66, 71, 75
kingship, xii, 57, 70, 72, 76, 87
land, xii–xiii, 2, 5, 8–9, 36, 61, 62n20, 93

Subject Index

of Canaan, 22–23, 26, 29–30, 43, 46–50, 57, 67, 79, 82–92
of Edom, 42–43
of Egypt, 51
and Sabbath, 51–55, 83–84, 95

Leviathan, 36–39, 87
light, 31, 33–34, 36, 38–39, 43, 60

millennialism, xiii, 21, 24
monotheism, 36n39, 37, 92

non-human(s), xiii, 7, 14–15, 22, 25n3, 27, 43, 49, 53, 60–61, 74, 96

obedience, 47n73, 48, 54, 73, 75, 81–83, 87
order, 22–23, 27, 29, 30, 35, 38, 40–48, 52–54, 58n21, 78, 87, 89–90
ordering, 22, 29–30, 38–39, 42–43, 49, 84, 94

planetary boundary(ies), 2–6
political, xi, 14, 18–19, 27, 91–92
Priestly (P) school, xii, 17, 22–23, 26–31, 34, 37–41, 45–46, 49, 51, 54, 56, 83–84, 86, 89–92

responsibility, xii–xiii, 12, 14, 17, 22–24, 25n2–3, 35, 38, 48, 51–53, 57, 72, 87, 90–93, 95
river, 64, 67–68, 70, 77, 91
royal status, 70–72

sabbath
  aetiology, xii, 26n11, 29–34

chaos and order, 35–39, 42–44
Christian ethics, 86, 88, 93–96
Israel keeping, 46–47, 52, 57, 75, 81–84
land keeping, xiii, 23, 49–55
temple, 22, 28, 30, 41–42, 45–48
sanctuary, xiii, 23, 28, 30, 46, 49, 55, 57, 66–70, 73–75, 80–86, 93–94
serpent, 71, 78, 83, 87
soil, 4, 15, 23, 43n62, 57, 61–62, 72, 74, 76–78, 82, 86–87, 93–94
sovereignty, divine/God, xii, 16–18, 22, 24, 38, 45, 65, 86, 92, 94

tabernacle, xii, 22–23, 30, 37n45, 41–42, 54, 69, 73–74, 80–81, 86, 91
temple, xii–xiii, 22–23, 29–30, 41, 45, 49, 54–57, 68–70, 74, 77, 81, 84, 86
Tiamat, 35–39, 87
Toledot, 27, 58–60, 62, 65
tree(s), 43, 62n20, 65, 69–70, 76, 83
  of life, 58n6, 69, 91

vomit(ing, ed), xiii, 23, 30, 52–53, 55, 84, 87

walk(s), 80–82
walking, 69, 80–82
water(s), 2–5, 33, 36–37, 40, 43, 64–65, 67–68, 77, 87, 90
wilderness, 36, 43, 62n20, 79–80
world, viii, xi, 5, 10, 15, 18–19, 25, 26n11, 50, 58, 77, 84, 87–90, 94

www.ingramcontent.com/pod-product-compliance
Lightning Source LLC
Chambersburg PA
CBHW050839160426
43192CB00011B/2082